Neon Vernacular

YUSEF

KOMUNYAKAA

Wesleyan University Press

Neon Vernacular

NEW AND

SELECTED POEMS

Yusef Komunyakaa

Published by University Press of New England / Hanover and London

Wesleyan University Press
Published by University Press of
New England, Hanover, NH 03755
Copyright © 1993 by Yusef Komunyakaa
All rights reserved
Printed in the United States of America
10 9 8 7 6
CIP data appear at the end of the book

The "New Poems" appeared in the following
magazines: Callaloo, Indiana Arts, The Iowa Review,
The Kenyon Review, The Louisville Review,
Mid-American Review, Ploughshares, Red Dirt,
River Styx, and The Southern Review.

Dedications & Other Darkhorses, Rocky Mountain
Creative Arts Journal, 1977; included by
permission. Lost in the Bonewheel Factory,
Lynx House Press, 1979; included by permission.
Copacetic, Wesleyan University Press, 1984;
included by permission. Toys in a Field,
Black River Press, 1986; included by permission.
I Apologize for the Eyes in My Head, Wesleyan
University Press, 1986; included by
permission. Dien Cai Dau, Wesleyan University
Press, 1988; included by permission.
February in Sydney, Matchbooks, 1989;
included by permission.

In memory of my grandmother, Mary,

and my father, J. W.

Contents

New Poems

Fog Galleon   3
At the Screen Door   4
Moonshine   5
Salt   6
Changes; or, Reveries at a Window Overlooking a Country Road,
    with Two Women Talking Blues in the Kitchen   8
Work   11
Praising Dark Places   13
A Good Memory   14
Birds on a Powerline   23
Fever   24
Little Man Around the House   27
Songs for My Father   28

from *Dedications & Other Darkhorses*

The Tongue Is   37
Chair Gallows   38
Translating Footsteps   39

from *Lost in the Bonewheel Factory*

Looking a Mad Dog Dead in the Eyes   43
1938   44
Stepfather: A Girl's Song   45
Apprenticeship   46
Light on the Subject   47
Beg Song   48
Passions   49
The Dog Act   51
For You, Sweetheart, I'll Sell Plutonium Reactors   52

The Nazi Doll 53
Corrigenda 54

from *Copacetic*

False Leads 57
Soliloquy: Man Talking to a Mirror 58
The Way the Cards Fall 59
Annabelle 60
Faith Healer 61
More Girl Than Boy 62
April Fools' Day 63
Untitled Blues 64
Back Then 65
Blasphemy 66
Safe Subjects 67
Black String of Days 69
Villon / Leadbelly 70
Elegy for Thelonious 71
Copacetic Mingus 72
Letter to Bob Kaufman 73
Woman, I Got the Blues 74
Newport Beach, 1979 75
Gloria's Clues 76
Charmed 77
The Cage Walker 78
Addendum 79
Epilogue to the Opera of Dead on Arrival 80
Blues Chant Hoodoo Revival 81

from *I Apologize for the Eyes in My Head*

Unnatural State of the Unicorn 87
Touch-up Man 88
How I See Things 89
The Thorn Merchant 90
The Thorn Merchant's Right-Hand Man 91
The Heart's Graveyard Shift 92
Boy Wearing a Dead Man's Clothes 94
The Music That Hurts 96
When in Rome—Apologia 97
The Thorn Merchant's Wife 99
The Thorn Merchant's Mistress 100
After Summer Fell Apart 102

The Brain to the Heart 104
Audacity of the Lower Gods 105
The Falling-Down Song 106
The Thorn Merchant's Son 107
I Apologize 108
1984 109
Dreambook Bestiary 113
Jonestown: More Eyes for *Jadwiga's Dream* 115
Landscape for the Disappeared 116
Good Joe 118
In the Background of Silence 120
For the Walking Dead 121
Child's Play 122
The Beast & Burden: Seven Improvisations 123

from *Toys in a Field*

Ambush 129
Monsoon Season 130
Water Buffalo 131
Le Xuan, Beautiful Spring 132
Please 133

from *Dien Cai Dau*

Camouflaging the Chimera 137
Tunnels 138
Starlight Scope Myopia 139
Hanoi Hannah 141
"You and I Are Disappearing" 142
Re-creating the Scene 143
We Never Know 145
A Break from the Bush 146
Tu Do Street 147
Communiqué 148
Prisoners 150
Jungle Surrender 152
Thanks 154
To Have Danced with Death 155
Report from the Skull's Diorama 156
Boat People 157
Missing in Action 158
Facing It 159

from *February in Sydney*

The Plea   163
The Man Who Carries the Desert Around Inside Himself:
   For Wally   165
Rocks Push   167
When Loneliness Is A Man   169
A Quality of Light   170
Gerry's Jazz   171
Boxing Day   173
Protection of Movable Cultural Heritage   175
Blue Light Lounge Sutra for the Performance Poets
   at Harold Park Hotel   176
February in Sydney   178

Neon
Vernacular

New Poems

Fog Galleon

Horse-headed clouds, flags
& pennants tied to black
Smokestacks in swamp mist.
From the quick green calm
Some nocturnal bird calls
Ship ahoy, ship ahoy!
I press against the taxicab
Window. I'm back here, interfaced
With a dead phosphorescence;
The whole town smells
Like the world's oldest anger.
Scabrous residue hunkers down under
Sulfur & dioxide, waiting
For sunrise, like cargo
On a phantom ship outside Gaul.
Cool glass against my cheek
Pulls me from the black schooner
On a timeless sea—everything
Dwarfed beneath the papermill
Lights blinking behind the cloudy
Commerce of wheels, of chemicals
That turn workers into pulp
When they fall into vats
Of steamy serenity.

At the Screen Door

Just before sunlight
Burns off morning fog.
Is it her, will she know
What I've seen & done,
How my boots leave little grave-stone
Shapes in the wet dirt,
That I'm no longer light
On my feet, there's a rock
In my belly? It weighs
As much as the story
Paul told me, moving ahead
Like it knows my heart.
Is this the same story
That sent him to a padded cell?
After all the men he'd killed in Korea
& on his first tour in Vietnam,
Someone tracked him down.
The Spec 4 he ordered
Into a tunnel in Cu Chi
Now waited for him behind
The screen door, a sunset
In his eyes, a dead man
Wearing his teenage son's face.
The scream that leaped
Out of Paul's mouth
Wasn't his, not this decorated
Hero. The figure standing there
Wasn't his son. Who is it
Waiting for me, a tall shadow
Unlit in the doorway, no more
Than an outline of the past?
I drop the duffle bag
& run before I know it,
Running toward her, the only one
I couldn't have surprised,
Who'd be here at daybreak
Watching a new day stumble
Through a whiplash of grass
Like a man drunk on the rage
Of being alive.

Moonshine

Drunken laughter escapes
Behind the fence woven
With honeysuckle, up to where
I stand. Daddy's running-buddy,
Carson, is beside him. In the time
It takes to turn & watch a woman
Tiptoe & pull a sheer blouse off
The clothesline, to see her sun-lit
Dress ride up peasant legs
Like the last image of mercy, three
Are drinking from the Mason jar.

That's the oak we planted
The day before I left town,
As if father & son
Needed staking down to earth.
If anything could now plumb
Distance, that tree comes close,
Recounting lost friends
As they turn into mist.

The woman stands in a kitchen
Folding a man's trousers—
Her chin tucked to hold
The cuffs straight.
I'm lonely as those storytellers
In my father's backyard
I shall join soon. Alone
As they are, tilting back heads
To let the burning ease down.
The names of women melt
In their mouths like hot mints,
As if we didn't know Old Man Pagget's
Stoopdown is doctored with
Slivers of Red Devil Lye.

Salt

Lisa, Leona, Loretta?
She's sipping a milkshake
In Woolworths, dressed in
Chiffon & fat pearls.
She looks up at me,
Grabs her purse
& pulls at the hem
Of her skirt. I want to say
I'm just here to buy
A box of Epsom salt
For my grandmama's feet.
Lena, Lois? I feel her
Strain to not see me.
Lines are now etched
At the corners of her thin,
Pale mouth. Does she know
I know her grandfather
Rode a white horse
Through Poplas Quarters
Searching for black women,
How he killed Indians
& stole land with bribes
& fake deeds? I remember
She was seven & I was five
When she ran up to me like a cat
With a gypsy moth in its mouth
& we played doctor & house
Under the low branches of a raintree
Encircled with red rhododendrons.
We could pull back the leaves
& see grandmama ironing
At their wide window. Once
Her mother moved so close
To the yardman we thought they'd kiss.

What the children of housekeepers
& handymen knew was enough
To stop biological clocks,
& it's hard now not to walk over
& mention how her grandmother
Killed her idiot son
& salted him down
In a wooden barrel.

Changes; or, Reveries at a Window Overlooking a Country Road, with Two Women Talking Blues in the Kitchen

Joe, Gus, Sham . . .
Even George Edward
Done gone. Done
Gone to Jesus, honey.
Doncha mean the devil,
Mary? Those Johnson boys
Were only sweet talkers
& long, tall bootleggers.
Child, now you can count
The men we usedta know
On one hand. They done
Dropped like mayflies—
Cancer, heart trouble,
Blood pressure, sugar,
You name it, Eva Mae.
Amen. Tell the truth,
Girl. I don't know.
Maybe the world's heavy
On their shoulders. Maybe
Too much bed hopping
& skirt chasing
Caught up with them.
God don't like ugly.
Look at my grandson
In there, just dragged in
From God only knows where,
He high tails it home
Inbetween women troubles.
He's nice as a new piece
Of silk. It's a wonder
Women don't stick to him
Like white on rice.
It's a fast world
Out there, honey.
They go all kinda ways.
Just buried John Henry
With that old guitar
Cradled in his arms.
Over on Fourth Street

Heat lightning jumpstarts the slow
afternoon & a syncopated rainfall
peppers the tinroof like Philly Joe
Jones' brushes reaching for a dusky
backbeat across the high hat. Rhythm
like cells multiplying . . . language &
notes made flesh. Accents & stresses,
almost sexual. Pleasure's knot; to wrestle
the mind down to unrelenting white space,
to fill each room with spring's contagious
changes. Words & music. "Ruby, My Dear"
turned down on the cassette player,
pulsates underneath rustic voices
waltzing out the kitchen—my grandmama
& an old friend of hers from childhood
talking B-flat blues. Time & space,
painful notes, the whole thing wrung
out of silence. Changes. Caesuras.
Nina Simone's downhome cry echoes
theirs—Mister Backlash, Mister Backlash—
as a southern breeze herds wild, blood-
red roses along the barbed-wire fence.
There's something in this house, maybe
those two voices & Satchmo's gold horn,
refracting time & making the Harlem
Renaissance live inside my head.
I can hear Hughes like a river
of fingers over Willie "The Lion" Smith's
piano, & some naked spiritual releases
a shadow in a reverie of robes & crosses.
Oriflamme & Judgment Day . . . undulant waves
bring in cries from Sharpeville & Soweto,
dragging up moans from shark-infested
seas as a blood moon rises. A shock
of sunlight breaks the mood & I hear
my father's voice growing young again,
as he says, "The devil's beating
his wife": One side of the road's rainy
& the other side's sunny. Imagination—

Singing 'bout hell hounds
When he dropped dead.
You heard 'bout Jack
Right? He just tilted over
In prayer meeting.
The good & the bad go
Into the same song.
How's Hattie? She
Still uppity & half
Trying to be white?
The man went off to war
& got one of his legs
Shot off & she wanted
To divorce him for that.
Crazy as a bessy bug.
Jack wasn't cold
In his grave before
She done up & gave all
The insurance money
To some young pigeon
Who never hit a lick
At work in his life.
He cleaned her out & left
With Donna Faye's girl.
Honey, hush. You don't
Say. Her sister,
Charlene, was silly
Too. Jump into bed
With anything that wore
Pants. White, black,
Chinese, crazy, or old.
Some woman in Chicago
hooked a blade into her.
Remember? Now don't say
You done forgot Charlene.
Her face a little blurred
But she coming back now.
Loud & clear. With those
Real big, sad, gray eyes.
A natural-born hellraiser,
& loose as persimmon pie.
You said it, honey.
Miss High Yellow.

driftwood from a spring flood, stockpiled
by Furies. Changes. Pinetop's boogiewoogie
keys stack against each other like syllables
in tongue-tripped elegies for Lady Day
& Duke. Don't try to make any sense
out of this; just let it take you
like Pres's tenor & keep you human.
Voices of school girls rush & surge
through the windows, returning
with the late March wind; the same need
pushing my pen across the page.
Their dresses lyrical against the day's
sharp edges. Dark harmonies. Bright
as lamentations behind a spasm band
from New Orleans. A throng of boys
are throwing at a bloodhound barking
near a blaze of witch hazel at the corner
of the fence. Mister Backlash.
I close my eyes & feel castanetted
fingers on the spine, slow as Monk's
"Mysterioso"; a man can hurt for years
before words flow into a pattern
so woman-smooth, soft as a pine-scented
breeze off the river Lethe. Satori-blue
changes. Syntax. Each naked string
tied to eternity—the backbone
strung like a bass. Magnolia
blossoms fall in the thick tremble
of Mingus's "Love Chant"; extended bars
natural as birds in trees & on powerlines
singing between the cuts—Yardbird
in the soul & soil. Boplicity
takes me to Django's gypsy guitar
& Dunbar's "broken tongue," beyond
god-headed jive of the apocalypse,
& back to the old sorrow songs
where boisterous flowers still nod on their
half-broken stems. The deep rosewood
of the piano says, "Holler
if it feels good." Perfect tension.
The mainspring of notes & extended
possibility—what falls on either side
of a word—the beat between & underneath.

I heard she's the reason
Frank shot down Otis Lee
Like a dog in The Blue
Moon. She was a blood-
Sucker. I hate to say this,
But she had Arthur
On a short leash too.
Your Arthur, Mary.
She was only a girl
When Arthur closed his eyes.
Thirteen at the most.
She was doing what women do
Even then. I saw them
With my own two eyes,
& promised God Almighty
I wouldn't mention it.
But it don't hurt
To mention it now, not
After all these years.

Organic, cellular space. Each riff & word
a part of the whole. A groove. New changes
created. "In the Land of Obladee"
burns out the bell with flatted fifths,
a matrix of blood & language
improvised on a bebop heart
that could stop any moment
on a dime, before going back
to Hughes at the Five Spot.
Twelve bars. Coltrane leafs through
the voluminous air for some note
to save us from ourselves.
The limbo & bridge of a solo . . .
trying to get beyond the tragedy
of always knowing what the right hand
will do . . . ready to let life play me
like Candido's drum.

Work

I won't look at her.
My body's been one
Solid motion from sunrise,
Leaning into the lawnmower's
Roar through pine needles
& crabgrass. Tiger-colored
Bumblebees nudge pale blossoms
Till they sway like silent bells
Calling. But I won't look.
Her husband's outside Oxford,
Mississippi, bidding on miles
Of timber. I wonder if he's buying
Faulkner's ghost, if he might run
Into Colonel Sartoris
Along some dusty road.
Their teenage daughter & son sped off
An hour ago in a red Corvette
For the tennis courts,
& the cook, Roberta,
Only works a half day
Saturdays. This antebellum house
Looms behind oak & pine
Like a secret, as quail
Flash through branches.
I won't look at her. Nude
On a hammock among elephant ears
& ferns, a pitcher of lemonade
Sweating like our skin.
Afternoon burns on the pool
Till everything's blue,
Till I hear Johnny Mathis
Beside her like a whisper.
I work all the quick hooks
Of light, the same unbroken
Rhythm my father taught me
Years ago: *Always give
A man a good day's labor.*
I won't look. The engine
Pulls me like a dare.
Scent of honeysuckle

Sings black sap through mystery,
Taboo, law, creed, what kills
A fire that is its own heart
Burning open the mouth.
But I won't look
At the insinuation of buds
Tipped with cinnabar.
I'm here, as if I never left,
Stopped in this garden,
Drawn to some Lotus-eater. Pollen
Explodes, but I only smell
Gasoline & oil on my hands,
& can't say why there's this bed
Of crushed narcissus
As if gods wrestled here.

Praising Dark Places

If an old board laid out in a field
Or backyard for a week,
I'd lift it up with a finger,
A tip of a stick.
Once I found a scorpion
Crimson as a hibernating crawfish
As if a rainbow edged underneath;
Centipedes & unnameable
Insects sank into loam
With a flutter. My first lesson:
Beauty can bite. I wanted
To touch scarlet pincers—
Warriors that never zapped
Their own kind, crowded into
A city cut off from the penalty
Of sunlight. The whole rotting
Determinism just an inch beneath
The soil. Into the darkness
Of opposites, like those racial
Fears of the night, I am drawn again,
To conception & birth. Roots of ivy
& farkleberry can hold a board down
To the ground. In this cellular dirt
& calligraphy of excrement,
Light is a god-headed
Law & weapon.

A Good Memory

I came to a bounty of black lustre
One July afternoon, & didn't
Call my brothers. A silence
Coaxed me up into oak branches
Woodpeckers had weakened.
But they held there, braced
By a hundred years of vines
Strong & thick
Enough to hang a man.
The pulpy, sweet musk
Exploded in my mouth
As each indigo skin collapsed.
Muscadines hung in clusters,
& I forgot about jellybeans,
Honeycomb, & chocolate kisses.
I could almost walk on air
The first time I couldn't get enough
Of something, & in that embrace
Of branches I learned the first
Secret I could keep.

Folk magic hoodooed us
Till the varmints didn't taste bitter
Or wild. We boys & girls
Knew how to cut away musk glands
Behind their legs. Good
With knives, we believed
We weren't poor. A raccoon
Would stand on its hind legs
& fight off dogs. Rabbits
Learned how to make hunters
Shoot at spiders when headlighting.
A squirrel played trickster
On the low branches
Till we were our own targets.
We garnished the animal's
Spirit with red pepper
& basil as it cooked

14   N E O N   V E R N A C U L A R

With a halo of herbs
& sweet potatoes. Served
On chipped, hand-me-down
Willow-patterned plates.
We weren't poor.
If we didn't say
Grace, we were slapped
At the table. Sometimes
We weighed the bullet
In our hands, tossing it left
To right, wondering if it was
Worth more than the kill.

       3   Breaking Ground
I told Mister Washington
You couldn't find a white man
With his name. But after forty years
At the tung oil mill, coughing up old dust,
He only talked butter beans & okra.
He moved like a sand crab.
Born half-broken, he'd say
If I didn't have this bad leg
I'd break ground to kingdom come.
He only stood erect behind
The plow, grunting against
The blade's slow cut.
Sometimes he'd just rock
Back & forth, in one place,
Hardly moving an inch
Till the dirt gave away
& he stumbled a foot forward,
Humming "Amazing Grace."
Like good & evil woven
Into each other, rutabagas
& Irish potatoes came out
Worm-eaten. His snow peas
Melted on tender stems,
Impersonating failure.
To prove that earth can heal,
He'd throw his body
Against the plow each day, pushing
Like a small man entering a big woman.

4 *Soft Touch*

Men came to her back door & knocked.
Food was the password. When switch engines
Stopped & boxcars changed tracks
To the sawmill, they came like Gypsies,
A red bandanna knotted at the throat,
A harmonica in the hip pocket of overalls
Thin as washed-out sky. They brought rotgut
Drought years, following some clear-cut
Sign or icon in the ambiguous
Green that led to her back porch
Like The Black Snake Blues.
They paid with yellow pencils
For crackling bread, molasses, & hunks
Of fatback. Sometimes grits & double-yolk
Eggs. Collard greens & okra. Louisianne
Coffee & chicory steamed in heavy white cups.
They sat on the swing & ate from blue
Flowered plates. Good-evil men who
Ran from something or to someone,
A thirty-year headstart on the Chicago hawk
That overtook them at Castle Rock.
She watched each one disappear over the trestle,
As if he'd turn suddenly & be her lost brother
Buddy, with bouquets of yellow pencils
In Mason jars on the kitchen windowsill.

5 *Shotguns*

The day after Christmas
Blackbirds lifted like a shadow
Of an oak, slow leaves
Returning to bare branches.
We followed them, a hundred
Small premeditated murders
Clustered in us like happiness.
We had the scent of girls
On our hands & in our mouths,
Moving like jackrabbits from one
Dream to the next. Brandnew
Barrels shone against the day
& stole wintery light
From trees. In the time it took
To run home & grab Daddy's gun,

The other wing-footed boys
Stumbled from the woods.
Johnny Lee was all I heard,
A siren in the flesh,
The name of a fallen friend
In their wild throats. Only Joe
Stayed to lift Johnny's head
Out of the ditch, rocking back
& forth. The first thing I did
Was to toss the shotgun
Into a winterberry thicket,
& didn't know I was running
To guide the paramedics into
The dirt-green hush. We sat
In a wordless huddle outside
The operating room, till a red light
Over the door began pulsing
Like a broken vein in a skull.

6   *Cousins*

Figs. Plums. Stolen
Red apples were sour
When weighed against your body
In the kitchen doorway
Where late July
Shone through your flowered dress
Worn thin by a hundred washings.
Like colors & strength
Boiled out of cloth,
Some deep & tall scent
Made the daylilies cower.
Where did the wordless
Moans come from in twilit
Rooms between hunger
& panic? Those years
We fought aside each other's hands.
Sap pulled a song
From the red-throated robin,
Drove bloodhounds mad
At the edge of a cornfield,
Split the bud down to hot colors.
I began reading you Yeats
& Dunbar, hoping for a potion

To draw the worm out of the heart.
Naked, unable or afraid,
We pulled each other back
Into our clothes.

    7 *Immigrants*
Lured by the cobalt
Stare of blast furnaces,
They talked to the dead
& unborn. Their demons
& gods came with black rhinoceros powder
In ivory boxes with secret
Latches that opened only
Behind unlit dreams.
They came as Guissipie, Misako,
& Goldberg, their muscles tuned
To the rhythm of meathooks & washboards.
Some wore raw silk,
A vertigo of color
Under sombrous coats,
& carried weatherbeaten toys.
They touched their hair
& grinned into locked faces
Of nightriders at the A & P.
Some darker than us, we taught them
About *Colored* water fountains & toilets
Before they traded sisters
& daughters for weak smiles
At the fish market & icehouse.
Gypsies among pines at nightfall
With guitars & cheap wine,
Sunsets orange as Django's
Cellophane bouquets. War
Brides spoke a few words of English,
The soil of distant lands
Still under their fingernails.
Ashes within urns. The Japanese plum
Fruitless in our moonlight.
Footprints & nightmares covered
With snow, we were way stations
Between sweatshops & heaven.
Worry beads. Talismans.
Passacaglia. Some followed

Railroads into our green clouds,
Searching for friends & sleepwalkers,
But stayed till we were them
& they were us, grafted in soil
Older than Jamestown & Osceola.
They lived in back rooms
Of stores in The Hollow,
Separated by alleyways
Leading to our back doors,
The air tasting of garlic.
Mister Cheng pointed to a mojo
High John the Conqueror & said
Ginseng. Sometimes zoot-suited
Apparitions left us talking
Pidgin Tagalog & Spanish.
We showed them fishing holes
& guitar licks. Wax pompadours
Bristled like rooster combs,
But we couldn't stop loving them
Even after they sold us
Rotting fruit & meat,
With fingers pressed down
On the scales. We weren't
Afraid of the cantor's snow wolf
Shadowplayed along the wall
Embedded in shards of glass.
Some came numbered. *Geyn
Tzum schvartzn yor.* Echoes
Drifted up the Mississippi,
Linking us to Sacco, Vanzetti,
& Leo Frank. Sometimes they stole
Our Leadbelly & Bessie Smith,
& headed for L.A. & The Bronx,
As we watched poppies bloom
Out of season, from a needle
& a hundred sanguine threads.

       8 *A Trailer at the Edge of a Forest*
A throng of boys whispered
About the man & his daughters,

How he'd take your five dollars
At the door. With a bull terrier

At his feet, he'd look on. Fifteen
& sixteen, Beatrice & Lysistrata

Were medicinal. Mirrors on the ceiling.
Posters of a black Jesus on a cross. Owls

& ravens could make a boy run out of his shoes.
Country & Western filtered through wisteria.

But I only found dead grass & tire tracks,
As if a monolith had stood there

A lifetime. They said the girls left quick
As katydids flickering against windowpanes.

> 9   *White Port & Lemon Juice*

At fifteen I'd buy bottles
& hide them inside a drainpipe
Behind the school
Before Friday-night football.
Nothing was as much fun
As shouldering a guard
To the ground on the snap,
& we could only be destroyed
By another boy's speed
On the twenty-yard line.

Up the middle on two, Joe.
Eddie Earl, you hit that damn
Right tackle, & don't let those
Cheerleaders take your eyes off
The ball. We knew the plays
But little about biology
& what we remembered about French
Was a flicker of blue lace
When the teacher crossed her legs.

Our City of Lights
Glowed when they darkened
The field at halftime
& a hundred freejack girls
Marched with red & green penlights
Fastened to their white boots

As the brass band played
"It Don't Mean A Thing."
They stepped so high.
The air tasted like jasmine.

We'd shower & rub
Ben-Gay into our muscles
Till the charley horses
Left. Girls would wait
Among the lustrous furniture
Of shadows, ready to
Sip white port & lemon juice.
Music from the school dance
Pulsed through our bodies
As we leaned against the brick wall:

Ernie K-Doe, Frogman
Henry, The Dixie Cups, & Little Richard.
Like echo chambers,
We'd du-wop song after song
& hold the girls in rough arms,
Not knowing they didn't want to be
Embraced with the strength
We used against fullbacks
& tight ends on the fifty.

Sometimes they rub against us,
Preludes to failed flesh,
Trying to kiss defeat
From our eyes. The fire
Wouldn't catch. We tried
To dodge the harvest moon
That grew red through trees,
In our Central High gold-
&-blue jackets, with perfect
Cleat marks on the skin.

10   The Woman Who Loved Yellow

Mud puppies at Grand Isle,
  English on cue balls, the war
    Somewhere in Southeast Asia—
      That's what we talked about
For hours. She wore a yellow blouse

& skin-tight hiphuggers,
    & would read my palm
        At the kitchen table: *Your lifeline*
Goes from here to here. Someday you'll fall
In love & swear you've been hoodooed.
    Mama Mary would look at us
        Out of the corner of an eye,
Or frame our faces in a pot lid
    She polished over & over. After she crossed
        The road, I'd throw a baseball
        Till my arms grew sore,
Floating toward flirtatious silhouettes.
    A few days home, her truck-driver
        Husband would blast a tree of mockingbirds
        With his shotgun, & then take off
For Motor City or Eldorado.
    She'd stand at our back door
        Like a dress falling open. Sometimes
        We'd go fishing at the millpond;
I kept away the snakes.
    We baited hooks with crickets.
        A forked willow branch
            Held two bamboo poles
As we unhooked the sky. Breasts
    & earlobes, every fingerprinted
        Curve. When we rose, goldenrod
            Left our tangled outline on the grass.

Birds on a Powerline

Mama Mary's counting them
Again. Eleven black. A single
Red one like a drop of blood

Against the sky. She's convinced
They've been there two weeks.
I bring her another cup of coffee

& a Fig Newton. I sit here reading
Frances Harper at the enamel table
Where I ate teacakes as a boy,

My head clear of voices brought back.
The green smell of the low land returns,
Stealing the taste of nitrate.

The deep-winter eyes of the birds
Shine in summer light like agate,
As if they could love the heart

Out of any wild thing. I stop,
With my finger on a word, listening.
They're on the powerline, a luminous

Message trailing a phantom
Goodyear blimp. I hear her say
Jesus, I promised you. Now

He's home safe, I'm ready.
My traveling shoes on. My teeth
In. I got on clean underwear.

Fever

I took orders, made my trail
Of blood, & you want me
To say it was right.
I go into the desert
Thistle, till I'm stopped
Like an obsidian statue.
The slow rise of below
Sea level to the Rockies,
Where I sleepwalk among
Headshops with false doors
Outside Red Rocks. I weigh my life
Against the evening sky
Orange as dinosaur dung
In scraggly ravines,
Before putting an ear to Cheyenne Mountain
To divine Ute horses,
Chief Joseph. Bombs rest
On springs to absorb a direct hit,
But I only hear my body
Talking to Venus. Breasts
Against the thinnest cloth
This side of heaven.
She rides a cloud horse,
Blowing a soundless whistle
Till I float off like a balloon
Cut loose. A ganglion
Of blossoms pushes through
April like a blood clot.
Odyssey in winding cells,
Into what divides & equals
The axis. Some nights I lie
Awake, staring into a promised land.
A cold wind out of Wyoming
Works the mind, like waves
Against stone, sand & willpower.
I don't know if I can ride
Out the slack, can just float
Along a precipice of indifference.
I can't trust my hands with loved ones,
The drum under my skin

Driven by a burning field. Trees
Stand like a death squad
Hemmed in by juniper & yucca.
Wanderlust, beds where
Unhealing is a religion.
I pray for those who work
Earth down to a blank stare
Up at the Colorado sky.
I thought I could learn
To hold these people, love
Their scary laughter & strength
With children & animals.
They accept heartworms
& infection like God,
Making me remember
That if I'd stayed home
I would've killed
Someone I love. My father
Stood apart, wounded
By what I had seen.
America, no brass bands,
No confetti. Please
Put away your pinwheels
& tin whistles. What I know
Now can lay open desire
With the right look.
Jill's perfume uncoils a noose
& I am rain beating a leaf;
Anita, a friend's wife, light
Burning paper, untying me
From the hot thread of a blues
Song. *Another man done gone*
Echoes from the prairie,
A penance flesh pays to doubt.
I can't outrun the throng
Of voices like a full moon
In a rearview mirror.
I want to be punched to the floor
In Hillbilly Heaven, as Luanne
Leans over the pool table
In a low-cut dress.
I know how to line up
The balls like a sniper

& not blink: breathe in,
Hold it till the heart
Slows down. The click
Of white ball against black
Like a kiss. In the Garden of the Gods
We make love under Pleiades,
With Balanced Rock
Gazing like an old mystic,
Where hundreds of birds
Flash in empty eyesockets.
Sugar Dee rolls in on her Harley
From Vegas, wearing silver boots
& gold tassels, & we lie
In each other's arms
Monday to Thursday. Linda,
Roma, Holly, Jan, Peaches—
I drain fears into them
But they can't raise the dead
In my eyes. The barbs fit
Like commas between names,
Worlds, ways of seeing.
If it wasn't for each daybreak
I'd stay here, staked like a star
In the back of the brain.
My shadow would keep watch
Where the coyote's loneliness
Shines like lice in fur.
Smoke edges into scrub oak
& aspen, & the map misleads
Like shark's teeth in the mountains.
I need to know simple things
Again, the hard facts
Alongside innocence.
You can hug flags into triangles,
But can't hide the blood
By tucking in the corners.
I can now see legs & arms
Wound in concertina wire,
The few who fell when I aimed.
One woman leads to the next
Excuse, names like teethmarks,
Everything connected to the sapper
With a grenade in his hand.

Little Man Around the House

Mama Elsie's ninety now.
She calls you whippersnapper.
When you two laugh, her rheumatism
Slips out the window like the burglar
She hears nightly. Three husbands
& an only son dead, she says
I'll always be a daddy's girl.
Sometimes I can't get Papa's face
Outta my head. But this boy, my great-
Great-grandson, he's sugar in my coffee.

You look up from your toy
Telescope, with Satchmo's eyes,
As if I'd put a horn to your lips.
You love maps of buried treasure,
Praying Mantis, & Public Enemy . . .
Blessed. For a moment, I'm jealous.
You sit like the king of trumpet
Between my grandmama & wife,
Youngblood, a Cheshire cat
Hoodooing two birds at once.

for Ladarius

Songs for My Father

I told my brothers I heard
You & mother making love,
Your low moans like a blues
Bringing them into the world.
I didn't know if you were laughing
Or crying. I held each one down
& whispered your song in their ears.
Sometimes I think they're still jealous
Of our closeness, having forgotten
We had to square-off & face each other,
My fists balled & cocked by haymakers.
That spring I lifted as many crossties
As you. They can't believe I can
Remember when you had a boy's voice.

     *

You were a quiet man
Who'd laugh like a hyena
On a hill, with your head
Thrown back, gazing up at the sky.
But most times you just worked
Hard, rooted in the day's anger
Till you'd explode. We always
Walked circles around
You, wider each year,
Hungering for stories
To save us from ourselves.
Like a wife who isn't touched,
We had to do something bad
Before you'd look into our eyes.

     *

We spent the night before Easter
Coloring eggs & piling them into pyramids
In two crystal punch bowls.
Our suits, ties, white shirts, shoes,
All lined up for the next day.
We had memorized our passages
From the bible, about the tomb
& the angel rolling back the stone.

You were up before daybreak,
In the sagebush, out among goldenrod
& mustard weed, hiding the eggs
In gopher holes & underneath roots.
Mother always argued with you,
Wondering why you made everything so hard.

    ❖

We stood on a wooden platform
Facing each other with sledgehammers,
A copper-tipped sieve sunken into the ground
Like a spear, as we threaded on five foot
Of galvanized pipe for the pump.
As if tuned to some internal drum,
We hammered the block of oak
Placed on top of the pipe.
It began inching downward
As we traded blows—one for you,
One for me. After a half hour
We threaded on another five foot. The sweat
Gleamed on our shirtless bodies, father
& son tied to each other till we hit water.

    ❖

Goddamn you. Goddamn you.
If you hit her again, I'll sail through
That house like a dustdevil.
Everyone & everything here
Is turning against you,
That's why I had to tie the dog
To a tree before you could chastise us.
He darted like lightning through the screen door.
I know you'll try to kill me
When it happens. You know
I'm your son & it's bound to happen.
Sometimes I close my eyes till I am
On a sea of falling dogwood blossoms,
But someday this won't work.

    ❖

I confess. I am the ringleader
Who sneaked planks out of the toolshed,
Sawed & hammered together the wagon.
But I wasn't fool enough to believe

That you would've loved our work.
So, my brothers & I dug a grave
In the corner of the field for our wagon
That ran smooth as a Nat King Cole
Love ballad. We'd pull it around
The edge of our world & rebury it
Before the 5 o'clock mill whistle blew.
I bet it's still there, the wood gray
& light as the ribs of my dog Red
After somebody gunned him down one night.

       ❉

You banged a crooked nail
Into a pine slab,
Wanting me to believe
I shouldn't have been born
With hands & feet
If I didn't do
Your kind of work.
You hated my books.
Sometimes at dusk,
I faced you like that
Childhood friend you trained
Your heart to always run
Against, the horizon crimson
As the eyes of a fighting cock.

       ❉

I never asked how you
Passed the driver's test,
Since you could only write
& read your name. But hell,
You were good with numbers;
Always counting your loot.
That Chevy truck swerved
Along back roads night & day.
I watched you use wire
& sunlight to train
The strongest limbs,
How your tongue never obeyed
The foreman, how the truck motor
Was stunted, frozen at sixty.

*

You wanted to fight
When I told you that a woman
Can get rid of a man
With a flake of lye
In his bread each day.
When you told her what I said
I bet the two of you made love
Till the thought flew out of your head.
Now, when you stand wax-faced
At the door, your eyes begging
Questions as you mouth wordless
Songs like a red-belly perch,
Assaying the scene for what it is,
I doubt if love can part my lips.

*

Sometimes you could be
That man on a red bicycle,
With me on the handlebars,
Just rolling along a country road
On the edge of July, honeysuckle
Lit with mosquito hawks.
We rode from under the shady
Overhang, back into sunlight.
The day bounced off car hoods
As the heat & stinking exhaust
Brushed against us like a dragon's
Roar, nudging the bike with a tremor,
But you steered us through the flowering
Dogwood like a thread of blood.

*

You lean on a yard rake
As dry leaves & grass smolder
In a ditch in mid March,
Two weeks before your sixty-first
Birthday. You say I look happy,
I must be in love. It is 1986,
Five months before your death.
You toss a stone at the two dogs
Hooked together in a corner of the yard.

You smile, look into my eyes
& say you want me to write you a poem.
I stammer for words. You
Toss another stone at the dogs
& resume raking the leafless grass.

＊

I never said thanks for Butch,
The wooden dog you pulled by a string.
It was ugly as a baldheaded doll.
Patched with wire & carpenter's glue, something
I didn't believe you had ever loved.
I am sorry for breaking it in half.
I never meant to make you go
Stand under the falling snowflakes
With your head bowed on Christmas
Day. I couldn't look at Butch
& see that your grandmother Julia,
The old slave woman who beat you
As if that's all she knew, had put love
Into it when she carved the dog from oak.

＊

I am unlike Kikuji
In Kawabata's *Thousand Cranes*,
Since I sought out one of your lovers
Before you were dead.
Though years had passed
& you were with someone else,
She thought I reminded her
Of a man she'd once known.
She pocketed the three dollars.
A big red lampshade bloodied
The room, as if held by a mad
Diogenes. Yes, she cried out,
But she didn't sing your name
When I planted myself in her.

＊

You spoke with your eyes
Last time I saw you, cramped
Between a new wife & the wall. You couldn't
Recognize funeral dirt stamped down
With dancesteps. Your name & features half

X-ed out. I could see your sex,
Your shame, a gold-toothed pout,
As you made plans for the next house you'd build,
Determined to prove me wrong. I never knew
We looked so much like each other. Before
I could say I loved you, you began talking money,
Teasing your will with a cure in Mexico.
You were skinny, bony, but strong enough to try
Swaggering through that celestial door.

Neon Vernacular

from *Dedications & Other Darkhorses*

The Tongue Is

xeroxed on brainmatter.
Grid-squares of words spread
like dirty oil over a lake.
The tongue even lies to itself,
gathering wildfire for songs of gibe.
Malcontented clamor, swish of reeds.
Slow, erratic, memory's loose
grain goes deep as water
in the savage green of oleander.
The tongue skips a beat, link of truth . . .
a chain running off a blue bicycle.
It starts like the slow knocking
in a radiator's rusty belly.
I enter my guilty plea
dry as the tongue of a beggar's
unlaced shoe. The tongue labors,
a victrola in the mad mouth-hole
of 3 A.M. sorrow.

Chair Gallows

Beating wind with a stick.
Riding herd on the human spirit.

It's how a man slips his head into a noose
& watches the easy weight of gods pull down

on his legs. I hope this is just another lie,
just another typo in a newspaper headline.

But I know war criminals
live longer than men lost between railroad tracks

& crossroad blues, with twelve strings
two days out of hock.

I've seen in women's eyes
men who swallow themselves in mirrors.

—memory of Phil Ochs

Translating Footsteps

She says Go fuck yourself
when I say Good-bye & good luck
with potted plants
under a granite moon.

A hand reaches from behind
to slash my throat.
Some things refuse translation:
the way I place my hands under
red silk to hear
a thin-skinned drum;
language of growing grass;
tombed treaties forgotten like lamps
left to burn out in a ghost town.

Each pause a clock inside stone . . .
digital, monumental as a grain
of wheat. Translate this
mojo song, footsteps
in a midnight hallway.

My doors enter from the sidestreet,
my windows painted basement black,
my mouth kisses the blues harp,
my heart hides like notes
locked in a cedar chest.

Neon Vernacular

from *Lost in the Bonewheel Factory*

Looking a Mad Dog Dead in the Eyes

Perception can force you to crawl
On God's great damn stone floor
& scrape your knees to the bone,
in love with the smooth round ass
of death. You've come to admire
that never-miss sniper on the rooftops.
The man who dances in circles
has fistbeaten a dog to the ground.
All the newsreel faces turn away
from the woman hanging naked
by her hair in a picture window,
as a scarecrow drags across a yellow field.
The young man with a nail in his foot
is your son, who believes
he's Christ, telling his father
what he wants to hear,
using a thorn for a toothpick.

1938

The granite-colored gulls unlocked
their wings & the door to a wall
swung open. Ghosts ducked through,
disappeared, so much spinal cord
looped & curved into spider darkness
hacked out of a calcium tomb,
where water screams back into you.
Each night became a red machine.

You were cornered in Paris, in the granary
where the raw brain snorted
like a blue horse & a moneysack
of hunger growled. Where shadows
of trees pulled your face down to kiss
stones. Each day murdered the black clock
of your voice, each day, each depravity
a pretty woman might throw her arms around,
knifed your shadow, Vallejo.
Death wore out your boot heels.

Stepfather: A Girl's Song

Again heavy rain drives him home
from the cornfield, washing away
footsteps & covering tracks.
For years his eyes undressed me.
There's a river in his stance
sweeping me away.

He comes into my bedroom
around corners of moonlight;
unexpected, he catches me
in his big arms. An ancient music
at the edge of my mouth.
He looks at me slantwise, warns:
"These hands whipped a mule crazy
& killed a man in '63."

My hands are like sparrows, stars
caught in tangled dance of branches.
He raises my clothes.
An undertow drags me down.
His mouth on mine, kissing my mother.

Apprenticeship

His fingernails are black
& torn from blows,
as if the hammer
declares its own angle of reference.
The young carpenter curses:
"Awww, fuck! Sonovabitch! Dumb shit!"

His girlfriend lowers her white dress,
then moves away.
She reappears nude,
props one foot upon a red chair,
looks him square in the eyes.
Her skin glistens like a woman
who's made love all afternoon.
Twenty-two stories up, he steps out
over the beams like a man with wings.

Light on the Subject

Hello, Mister Jack
The Ripper, come on in
make yourself at home.
Here in Deadwood City
your hands are clean as ours.
Our eyes flash back to
knives on silver whetstones.
Can I get you anything, partner?
Perhaps a shot of Four Roses?
In this gray station of wood
our hearts are wet rags
& we turn to ourselves,
holding our own hands
as the scaffolds sway.
I can tell you this much
Brother Justice, our faith's
unshakable, even if we rock stones
asleep in broken arms.
We've all seen moonlight on lakes
& crows whittled from a block
of air. In this animal-night, no
siree, we won't disappoint you
when we rise out of hawkweed,
because we still have
a thing about Law
& Order.

Beg Song

. . . where geometry borders on dream, and where the
duende wears a muse's mask for the eternal punishment
of the great king.   —Federico Garcia Lorca

Foolhearted mindreader,
help us see how
the heart begs,
how fangs of opprobrium
possess our eyes. Truth
serum: how the index finger works
up into love, how the greased hand
slides up the wombholler of madness
& rebirth, whispering:
Look, back of the eyes. Each
gazes into its fish heart, final mirror
of beauty & monkeyshine.
Run your tongue along
fear in the frontal lobe.
Introduce us to that crazy man
with his face buried
in your hands.
In the slack bed, meat
falls through the door
of itself. Soul of a lamp.
Slipshod genius, show us
the cutworm's silly heart,
how the telescopic love-eye
probes back to its genesis.

Passions

Coitus
Ah, pink tip of sixth sense,
oyster fat of lovepearl,
dew-seed & singing leaf-tongue,
lizard's head of pure thought.

Body Painting
To step into the golden lute
& paint one's soul
on the body. Bird
goddess & slow snake
in the flowered tree. Circle,
lineage, womb, mouth, leaf-footed
godanimal on a man's chest
who leaps into the moon
on a woman's belly.

Blue-green Iridescent Flies
Meat, excrement, a source
of life attracts this
message & definition
of the ultimate us.
They fly off
with the weight of the world.

Peepshow
A new moon rises
on an elevator over the mountain.

String Bass
The moon's at the window,
as she rocks in the arms
of this lonely player
like a tall Yoruba woman.

Pinball Machines
Encased in glass, a woman
opens her eyes. The room floods
with a century of bells.
Magnetic balls & sound of metal
seem enough to build a locomotive
moving through the room's wooden bones.

Butterflies
Incandescent anthologies
semi-zoological alphabets of fire,
these short lives transmigrate, topaz
memories cling to air, release wordflesh
from the cocoon of silk fear.

Psilocybe
One hundred purple rooms
in a mirror of black water.
I must enter each,
interrogated by a different demon.
In the distance I can hear
the sea coming. A woman at Laguna Beach.
Her eyes now seashells.
Her arms two far-off sails.
Like a tree drags the ground on a windy day
with yellow & red fruit too soft to eat,
she comes toward me. Stars cluster
her laughter like a nest of moth eyes—
her focus on the world.
The closer she comes, the deeper
I work myself away into music
that I hope can save us both.
A man steps from a junkyard of chrome
fenders & hubcaps,
pulling off masks.
At least a hundred scattered about.
The last one: I'm him.

The Dog Act

I'm the warm-up act.
I punch myself in the face
across the makeshift stage.
Fall through imaginary trapdoors.
Like the devil, I turn cartwheels
& set my hair afire.
Contradiction, the old barker
drunk again on these lights
& camaraderie. The white poodles,
Leo, Camellia, St. John, & Anna,
leap through fiery hoops
to shake my hand.
I make a face
that wants to die
inside me.
"Step right up ladies & gentlemen,
see the Greatest Show on Earth,
two-headed lions, seraphim,
unicorns, satyrs, a woman
who saws herself in half."
I can buckdance till I am
in love with the trapeze artist.
Can I have your attention now?
I'm crawling across the stagefloor
like a dog with four broken legs.
You're supposed to jump up
& down now, laugh & applaud.

For You, Sweetheart, I'll Sell Plutonium Reactors

For you, sweetheart, I'll ride back down
into black smoke early Sunday morning
cutting fog, grab the moneysack
of gold teeth. Diamond mines
soil creep groan ancient cities, archaeological
diggings, & yellow bulldozers turn around all night
in blood-lit villages. Inhabitants here once gathered seashells
that glimmered like pearls. When the smoke clears, you'll see
an erected throne like a mountain to scale,
institutions built with bones, guns hidden in walls
that swing open like big-mouthed B-52s.
Your face in the mirror is my face. You tapdance
on tabletops for me, while corporate bosses
arm wrestle in back rooms for your essential downfall.
I entice homosexuals into my basement butcher shop.
I put my hands around another sharecropper's throat
for that mink coat you want from Saks Fifth,
short-change another beggarwoman,
steal another hit song from Sleepy
John Estes, salt another gold mine in Cripple Creek,
drive another motorcycle up a circular ice wall,
face another public gunslinger like a bad chest wound,
just to slide hands under black silk.
Like the Ancient Mariner steering a skeleton ship
against the moon, I'm their hired gunman
if the price is right, take a contract on myself.
They'll name mountains & rivers in my honor.
I'm a drawbridge over manholes for you, sweetheart.
I'm paid two hundred grand
to pick up a red telephone anytime & call up God.
I'm making tobacco pouches out of the breasts of Indian maidens
so we can stand in a valley & watch grass grow.

The Nazi Doll

It sits lopsided
in a cage. Membrane.

Vertebra. This precious, white
ceramic doll's brain

twisted out of a knob of tungsten.
It bleeds a crooked smile

& arsenic sizzles in the air.
Its eyes an old lie.

Its bogus tongue, Le Diable.
Its lampshade of memory.

Guilt yahoos, benedictions
in its Cro-Magnon skull

blossom, a flurry of fireflies,
vowels of rattlesnake beads.

Its heart hums the song of dust
like a sweet beehive.

Corrigenda

I take it back.
The crow doesn't have red wings.
They're pages of dust.
The woman in the dark room
takes the barrel of a .357 magnum
out of her mouth, reclines
on your bed, a Helena Rubinstein smile.
I'm sorry, you won't know your father
by his darksome old clothes.
He won't be standing by that tree.
I haven't salted the tail
of the sparrow.
Erase its song from this page.
I haven't seen the moon
fall open at the golden edge of our sleep.
I haven't been there
like the tumor in each of us.
There's no death that can
hold us together like twin brothers
coming home to bury their mother.
I never said there's a book inside
every tree. I never said I know how
the legless beggar feels when
the memory of his toes itch.
If I did, drunkenness
was then my god & naked dancer.
I take it back.
I'm not a suicidal mooncalf;
you don't have to take my shoelaces.
If you must quote me, remember
I said that love heals from inside.

from *Copacetic*

False Leads

Hey! Mister Bloodhound Boss,
I hear you're looking for Slick Sam
the Freight Train Hopper.
They tell me he's a crack shot.
He can shoot a cigarette out of a man's mouth
thirty paces of an owl's call.
This morning I glimpsed red
against that treeline.
Aïe, aïe, mo gagnin toi.
Wise not to let night catch you out there.
You can get so close to a man
you can taste his breath.
They say Slick Sam's a mind reader:
he knows what you gonna do
before you think it.
He can lead you into quicksand
under a veil of swamp gas.
Now you know me, Uncle T,
I wouldn't tell you no lie.
Slick Sam knows these piney woods
& he's at home here in cottonmouth country.
Mister, your life could be worth
less than a hole in a plug nickel.
I bet old Slick Sam knows
about bloodhounds & black pepper—
how to put a bobcat into a crocus sack.

Soliloquy: Man Talking to a Mirror

Working night shift
    panhandling Larimer Square
ain't been easy.
        A pair of black brogans
can make a man
limp badly.
        Lawd, this flophouse
        has a hangover—
        you just can't
love hard knowledge
    this way, Buddy Boy.
        Big shouldered,
            you're still a born pushover,
        a tree climber
        in the devil's skull.
You hide behind panes
of unwashed light,
        grazing with stubborn goats.
        Mister Big Shot,
            once you dredged down
        years towards China
but didn't find
a pot of gold—
        chopped down a forest of doors
& told deadly machines
where to go.
            Now you're counting taverns,
            dumbfounded
by a hunk of oily keys
    to foul weather.
        Tangled in the bell ropes
        of each new day,
scribbling on the bottom line
        of someone else's dream,
        loitering
            in public courtyards
telling statues where to fall.

The Way the Cards Fall

Why did you stay away
so long? I've buried another
husband, since I last saw you
holding to the horizon.
I hear where you now live
it snows year-round.
The pear & apple trees
have even missed you—
dead branches scattered
about like war. Come closer,
my eyes have grown night-dim.
Across the field white boxes
of honeybees silent as dirt,
silent as your missent
postcards. Evening
sunlight's faded my hair,
the old stable's slouched
to the ground. I dug a hole
for that calico, Cyclops,
two years ago. Now
milkweed & blackberries
are keepers of the cornfield.
That's how the cards fall;
& Anna, that beautiful girl
you once loved enough
to die over & over again for,
now lives in New Orleans
on both sides
of Bourbon Street.

Annabelle

My head hangs.
It's all to do with
a woman back in Alabama.
All to do with Annabelle
hugging every road sign
between here & Austin, Texas.
All to do with rope & blood.

He's all to do with America.
All to do with all the No-Dick
Joneses. Mornings shattered.
Crickets mourn—
sing out of genetic code.

All to do with shadows
kneeling in the woods.
All to do with inherited iron maidens.
Beg for death in the womb.
Beg for it inside skulls—flower,
dust, lilac perfume, cold fire.

Gonna get lowdown tonight.

Faith Healer

Come singing in your chains,
Sweet Daughter. Dance, yes.
All the light-fingered artisans
of sacrilege, of wishful thinking
who failed, all the goat-footed heretics
crying for a High John the Conqueror
root, now here you are,
dear child, naked facing God.

A laying on of hands. Yes,
walk out of the grave whole.
Blood on the thorns. *Vox*
& *ossa*. You're here, girl,
to obey His design in the flesh.
I plant a kiss where it hurts.
Trees walk forth. Throw away
your sticks & lean on Jesus.

Touch my hand, touch my hand!

More Girl Than Boy

You'll always be my friend.
Is that clear, Robert Lee?
We go beyond the weighing
of each other's words,
hand on a shoulder,
go beyond the color of hair.
Playing Down the Man on the Field
we embraced each other before
I discovered girls.
You taught me a heavy love
for jazz, how words can hurt
more than a quick jab.
Something there's no word for
saved us from the streets.

Night's pale horse
rode you past common sense,
but you made it home from Chicago.
So many dreams dead.
All the man-sweet gigs
meant absolutely nothing.
Welcome back to earth, Robert.
You always could make that piano
talk like somebody's mama.

April Fools' Day

They had me laid out in a white
satin casket. What the hell
went wrong, I wanted to ask.
Whose midnight-blue sedan
mowed me down, what unnameable fever
bloomed amber & colchicum
in my brain, which doctor's scalpel
slipped? Did it happen
on a rainy Saturday, blue
Monday, Vallejo's Thursday?
I think I was on a balcony
overlooking the whole thing.
My soul sat in a black chair
near the door, sullen
& no-mouthed. I was fifteen
in a star-riddled box,
in heaven up to my eyelids.
My skin shone like damp light,
my face was the gray of something
gone. They were all there.
My mother behind an opaque veil,
so young. My brothers huddled like stones,
my sister rocked her Shirley Temple
doll to sleep. Three fat ushers fanned
my grandmamas, used smelling salts.
All my best friends—Cowlick,
Sneaky Pete, Happy Jack, Pie Joe,
& Comedown Jones.
I could smell lavender,
a tinge of dust. Their mouths,
palms of their hands
stained with mulberries.
Daddy posed in his navy-blue suit
as doubting Thomas: some twisted
soft need in his eyes, wondering if
I was just another loss
he'd divided his days into.

Untitled Blues   *after a photograph by Yevgeni Yevtushenko*

I catch myself trying
to look into the eyes
of the photo, at a black boy
behind a laughing white mask
he's painted on. I
could've been that boy
years ago.
Sure, I could say
everything's copacetic,
listen to a Buddy Bolden cornet
cry from one of those coffin-
shaped houses called
shotgun. We could
meet in Storyville,
famous for quadroons,
with drunks discussing God
around a honky-tonk piano.
We could pretend we can't
see the kitchen help
under a cloud of steam.
Other lurid snow jobs:
night & day, the city
clothed in her see-through
French lace, as pigeons
coo like a beggar chorus
among makeshift studios
on wheels—Vieux Carré
belles having portraits painted
twenty years younger.
We could hand jive
down on Bourbon & Conti
where tap dancers hold
to their last steps,
mammy dolls frozen
in glass cages. The boy
locked inside your camera,
perhaps he's lucky—
he knows how to steal
laughs in a place
where your skin
is your passport.

Back Then

I've eaten handfuls of fire
back to the bright sea
of my first breath
riding the hipbone of memory
& saw a wheel of birds
a bridge into the morning
but that was when gold
didn't burn out a man's eyes
before auction blocks
groaned in courtyards
& nearly got the best of me
that was when the spine
of every ebony tree wasn't
a pale woman's easy chair
black earth-mother of us all
crack in the bones & sombre
eyes embedded like beetles
in stoic heartwood
seldom have I needed
to shake a hornet's nest
from the breastplate
fire over the ground
pain tears me to pieces
at the pottery wheel
of each dawn
an antelope leaps
in the heartbeat
of the talking drum

Blasphemy*

You named those lies clustered
in each rib cage. Attached
to some circular truth, you
glimpsed soldiers of fortune
sweeping their footprints
with branches of mistletoe.
You showed them the corpse garden
couldn't keep blooming,
not forever—black bags
of songs split open at sunrise.
You copied down the earthworm's
calligraphy, broke illusion's hymen,
uncovered the scars smiling
under Dutch silk, translated
the hyena's soliloquy.
You carbon-dated the skull
paperweight on the commissioner's desk
& filled in with charcoal
these mental lapses—
when all the gone ones
resurfaced as dancing rags
in the wind, you named
the beast upon the gallows tree,
its sag-belly dragging
the ground. You appraised
the medieval rot taking hold
of dirt floors, crawling up
the cathedral's high rafters.
Madness, you brought it home.

*Harold Rubin was tried for blasphemy on the basis
of his artwork and exiled from South Africa.

Safe Subjects

How can love heal
the mouth shut this way?
Say something worth breath.
Let it surface, recapitulate
how fat leeches press down
gently on a sex goddess's eyelids.
Let truth have its way with us
like a fishhook holds
to life, holds dearly to nothing
worth saying—pull it out,
bringing with it hard facts,
knowledge that the fine underbone
of hope is also attached
to inner self, underneath it all.
Undress. No, don't be afraid
even to get Satan mixed up in this
acknowledgement of thorns:
meaning there's madness
in the sperm, in the egg,
fear breathing in its blood sac,
true accounts not so easily
written off the sad book.

Say something about pomegranates.
Say something about real love.
Yes, true love—more than
parted lips, than parted legs
in sorrow's darkroom of potash
& blues. Let the brain stumble
from its hidingplace, from its cell block,
to the edge of oblivion
to come to itself, sharp-tongued
as a boar's grin in summer moss
where a vision rides the back
of God, at this masquerade.
Redemptive as a straight razor
against a jugular vein—
unacknowledged & unforgiven.
It's truth we're after here,
hurting for, out in the streets

where my brothers kill each other,
each other's daughters & guardian angels
in the opera of dead on arrival.

Say something that resuscitates
us, behind the masks,
as we stumble off into neon nights
to loveless beds & a second skin
of loneliness. Something political as dust
& earthworms at work in the temple
of greed & mildew, where bowed lamps
cast down shadows like blueprints of graves.
Say something for us who can't believe
in the creed of nightshade.
Yes, say something to us dreamers
who decode the message of dirt
between ancient floorboards
as black widow spiders
lay translucent eggs
in the skull of a dead mole
under a dogwood in full bloom.

Black String of Days

Tonight I feel the stars are out
to use me for target practice.
I don't know why
they zero in like old
business, each a moment of blood
unraveling forgotten names.
This world of dog-eat-dog
& anything goes.
On the black string of days
there's an unlucky number
undeniably ours.
As the Milky Way
spreads out its map
of wounds, I feel
like a snail on a salt lick.
What can I say? Morning's crow
poses on a few sticks, a cross
dressed in Daddy's work shirt—
how its yellow eyes shine.
It knows I believe
in small things.
I dig my fingers into wet dirt
where each parachute seed pod
matters. Some insect
a fleck of fool's gold.
I touch it,
a man asking for help
as only he knows how.

Villon/Leadbelly

Two bad actors canonized by ballads
flowering into dusk, crowned with hoarfrost.
But the final blows weren't dealt in Meung-
sur-Loire or the Angola pen. "Irene,
Irene, I'll see you in my dreams."

Unmoved by the hangman's leer,
these two roughhouse bards ignored
his finger traveling down the list.
They followed every season's penniless
last will & testament. Their songs

bleed together years. A bridge,
more than a ledger of bones.
Ghosts under the skin in bedlam,
Princes of Fools, they prowled
syncopated nights of wolfbane

& gin mills of starlight
at The Golden Mortar & The Bucket
of Blood, double-daring men across
thresholds, living down the list,
strung out on immortality's rag.

Elegy for Thelonious

Damn the snow.
Its senseless beauty
pours a hard light
through the hemlock.
Thelonious is dead. Winter
drifts in the hourglass;
notes pour from the brain cup.
Damn the alley cat
wailing a muted dirge
off Lenox Ave. ·
Thelonious is dead.
Tonight's a lazy rhapsody of shadows
swaying to blue vertigo
& metaphysical funk.
Black trees in the wind.
Crepuscule with Nelly
plays inside the bowed head.
"Dig the Man Ray of piano!"
O Satisfaction,
hot fingers blur
on those white rib keys.
Coming on the Hudson.
Monk's Dream.
The ghost of bebop
from 52nd Street,
footprints in the snow.
Damn February.
Let's go to Minton's
& play "modern malice"
till daybreak. Lord,
there's Thelonious
wearing that old funky hat
pulled down over his eyes.

Copacetic Mingus

"'Mingus One, Two and Three.
Which is the image you want the world to see?'"
—Charles Mingus, *Beneath the Underdog*

Heartstring. Blessed wood
& every moment the thing's made of:
ball of fatback
licked by fingers of fire.
Hard love, it's hard love.
Running big hands down
the upright's wide hips,
rocking his moon-eyed mistress
with gold in her teeth.
Art & life bleed
into each other
as he works the bow.
But tonight we're both a long ways
from the Mile High City,
1973. Here in New Orleans
years below sea level,
I listen to *Pithecanthropus
Erectus*: Up & down, under
& over, every which way—
thump, thump, dada—ah, yes.
Wood heavy with tenderness,
Mingus fingers the loom
gone on Segovia,
dogging the raw strings
unwaxed with rosin.
Hyperbolic bass line. Oh, no!
Hard love, it's hard love.

Letter to Bob Kaufman

The gold dust of your voice
& twenty-five cents
can buy a cup of coffee.
We sell pain for next to nothing! Nope,
you don't know me but your flesh-
&-blood language lingers in my head
like treason & raw honey.
I read *GOLDEN SARDINE*
& dance the Calinda
to come to myself.
Needles, booze, high-steppers
with dangerous eyes.
Believe this, brother,
we're dice in a hard time hustle.
No more than handfuls of meat.
C'mon, play the dozens,
you root worker & neo-hoodooist,
you earth lover & hole-card peeper.
We know roads dusty with old griefs
& hot kiss joys.
Bloodhounds await ambush.
Something, perhaps the scent
of love, draws them closer.

Woman, I Got the Blues

I'm sporting a floppy existential sky-blue hat
when we meet in the Museum of Modern Art.

Later, we hold each other
with a gentleness that would break open
ripe fruit. Then we slow-drag
to Little Willie John, we bebop
to Bird LPs, bloodfunk, lungs paraphrased
till we break each other's fall.
For us there's no reason the scorpion
has to become our faith healer.

Sweet Mercy, I worship
the curvature of your ass.
I build an altar in my head.
I kiss your breasts & forget my name.

Woman, I got the blues.
Our shadows on floral wallpaper
struggle with cold-blooded mythologies.
But there's a stillness in us
like the tip of a magenta mountain.
Half-naked on the living-room floor;
the moon falling through the window
on you like a rapist.

Your breath's a dewy flower stalk
leaning into sweaty air.

Newport Beach, 1979

To them I'm just a crazy nigger
out watching the ocean
drag in silvery nets of sunfish,
dancing against God's spine—
if He's earth, if He's a hunk of celestial bone,
if He's real as Superman
holding up the San Andreas Fault.

Now look, Miss Baby Blue Bikini,
don't get me wrong.
I'm not the Redlight Bandit,
not Mack the Knife, or Legs Diamond
risen from the dead
in a speak-easy of magenta sunsets perpetually
overshadowing nervous breakdowns.

I'm just here where first-degree eyes
look at me like loaded dice,
as each day hangs open
in hurting light like my sex
cut away & tied to stalks
of lilies, with nothing else
left to do for fun.

Gloria's Clues

Whenever we're left alone in the room she performs.
Sucking on a lemon-yellow lollipop, she goes for the
heart. When she pulls her panties down I turn my eyes
to the blond Jesus glowing on the wall. Some dance
propels her across the floor. When Gabe & Annabelle
return from the kitchen, she's back playing with her
ABC blocks, all twelve colors stacked into a pyramid.
We shuffle the bones, we slap 'em down: blank to
blank, five to five. We get the right rhythm going & it
sounds like a punch press at the mill, minutes fly like
metal shards from a lathe. Gloria plays with her life-
size doll that closes its eyes. With peripheral vision I
see her sneak a cigarette from the clamshell ashtray—
a slow kiss of burns bubbles around the doll's belly-
button. I wonder if it's all in my head. The bones rain
down like blows against the oak tabletop. Tequila
Sunrises & San Miguels work us over, while outside
snowflakes accumulate on Dutch elms. Finally the
game winds down to Gabe's smile as he tallies points—
"the damage" we've done to each other tonight. I
tell them it's a nice walk six blocks through the snow.
No, no, I'm not drunk. Annabelle stands where the
doorway's heavy light falls through her white muslin
dress like sad wisdom. An induced schizophrenia—
we look at each other without looking. Gloria's green
eyes follow me out the door into the street. I don't
know where my feet are headed.

Charmed

I jump between the cat
& a bird. The cat cries
as though I had struck her with a stick.
If animals possess souls
her cry's close to sin.
She moves toward the bird.
Women have moved gently
toward me—& me toward them—
this way. Some dance
concealed under the skin,
creatures of habit.
The bird sits perfectly lost
like a flower. So red.
Lost behind the five colors
of the cat's eyes brighter
than truest memory of water.
The cat has pierced him
deeper than bad luck,
moving like a hand buried
in the dark. Years ago
I stepped between a woman & man
at each other's throat,
both turning against me.
I try to shoo the bird away.
I pick him up & his small heart
flutters through me.
The bird has no song left.
I close my eyes,
I place him on the ground,
I back away.

The Cage Walker

He shoves the .38
into his coat pocket
& walks back into
the dark. Night
takes him like a conveyer belt.

For a split second
he's been there
in the ditch,
hood pulled from over a death's-head.

He sits on a park bench.
Blue uniform behind every elm,
night sticks. He thinks how a man
enters the deeper, darker machine.

His fingers touch gun metal.
He stands & walks down
toward the wharf; ships rock
in white foghorn silence.
Water slams, steel doors
closing in a tunnel.

The quarter-moon goes blank
behind a cloud. He frames a picture
in his head, retraces footsteps
to Shorty's Liquor Store.
He will go in this time.

He stands under a street lamp.
Moths float by
& he counts cars:
1, 2, 3, 4, 5, aw shit.

A woman walks past & smiles.
Her red dress turns the corner
like blood in a man's eyes.
He stares at his hands.
They say August is a good time
for a man to go crazy.

Addendum

I'm a bone roller,
a high roller,
listening to Lester Young
& Big Mama Thornton,
Peacock 1612.

I'm a street nigger
from way back when: I am
multilateral
extended metaphors
for cellblock blues
& Cat-Eye balling the jack.

I'm a womb-scratcher.
I'm a double-dealer.
I'm the chance you take
with the past tonight.

Epilogue to the Opera of Dead on Arrival

I can still sing
"Ain't Goin' Down to the Well
No Mo' " like Leadbelly.
Blow out the candles
& start all anew.
Where's Sweet Luck?—
a kiss from that woman.
It's the way starlight
struck the blade. If only
I could push down on her chest
& blow a little breath
into her mouth, maybe.
Handcuff me, slam my head
against bars of the jailhouse,
use your blackjacks,
zero in on my weaknesses,
let enough melancholy
to kill a mule
settle into my lungs.

my story is
how deep the heart runs
to hide & laugh
with your hands
over your blank mouth
face behind the mask
talking in tongues
something tearing
feathers from a crow
that screams
from the furnace
the black candle
in a skull
sweet pain of meat

> let's pour the river's rainbow
> into our stone water jars
> bad luck isn't red flowers
> crushed under jackboots

your story is
a crippled animal
dragging a steel trap
across desert sand
a bee's sting inside your heart
& its song of honey
in my groin
a factory of blue jays
in honey locust leaves
wet pages of smoke
like a man
deserting his shadow
in dark woods
the dog that limps away
& rotten fruit on the trees
this story is
the speaking skull
on the mantelpiece
the wingspan of a hawk
at the edge of a coyote's cry

the seventh son's mojo hand
holding his life together
with a black cat bone
the six grandfathers
& spider woman
the dust wings
of ghost dance vision
deer that can't
stand for falling
wunmonije witch doctor
backwater blues
juju man
a silk gown on the floor
a black bowl
on a red lacquered table
x-rated
because it's true

    let's pour starlight
    from our stone water jars
    pain isn't just red flowers
    crushed under jackboots

my story is
inside a wino's bottle
the cup blood leaps into
eight-to-the-bar
a man on his knees
facing the golden calf
the silverfish of old lust
mama hoodoo
a gullah basket
woven from your hair
love note from the madhouse
thornbushes
naming the shape
of things to come
old murder weapons
strings of piano wire

    let's pour the night
    into our stone water jars
    this song isn't red flowers
    crushed under silence

our story is
a rifle butt
across our heads
arpeggio of bowed grass
among glass trees
where they kick down doors
& we swan-dive from
the brooklyn bridge
a post-hypnotic suggestion
a mosaic membrane
skin of words
mirrors shattered
in roadhouses
in the gun-barrel night
how a machine moves
deeper into piles
of bones
the way we
crowd at the foot
of the gallows

Neon Vernacular

from *I Apologize for the Eyes in My Head*

Unnatural State of the Unicorn

Introduce me first as a man.
Don't mention superficial laurels
the dead heap up on the living.
I am a man. Cut me & I bleed.
Before embossed limited editions,
before fat artichoke hearts marinated
in rich sauce & served with imported wines,
before antics & Agnus Dei,
before the stars in your eyes
mean birth sign or Impression,
I am a man. I've scuffled
in mudholes, broken teeth in a grinning skull
like the moon behind bars. I've done it all
to be known as myself. No titles.
I have principles. I won't speak
on the natural state of the unicorn
in literature or self-analysis.
I have no birthright to prove,
no insignia, no secret
password, no fleur-de-lis.
My initials aren't on a branding iron.
I'm standing here in unpolished
shoes & faded jeans, sweating
my manly sweat. Inside my skin,
loving you, I am this space
my body believes in.

Touch-up Man

I playact the three monkeys
carved over the lintel of a Japanese shrine,
mouthing my mantra: *I do*
what I'm told. I work
from Mr. Pain's notecards;
he plants the germ of each idea.
And I'm careful not to look
at his private secretary's legs,
as I turn the harvest through the dumb-mill
of my hands. Half-drunk
with my tray of bright tools,
I lean over the enlarger,
in the light table's chromatic glare
where I'm king, doctoring photographs,
airbrushing away the corpses.

How I See Things

I hear you were
sprawled on the cover of *Newsweek*
with freedom marchers, those years
when blood tinted the photographs,
when fire leaped into the trees.

Negatives of nightriders
develop in the brain.
The Strawberry Festival Queen
waves her silk handkerchief,
executing a fancy high kick

flashback through the heart.
Pickups with plastic Jesuses
on dashboards head for hoedowns.
Men run twelve miles into wet cypress
swinging bellropes. Ignis fatuus can't be blamed

for the charred Johnson grass.
Have we earned the right
to forget, forgive
ropes for holding
to moonstruck branches?

Every last stolen whisper
the hoot owl echoes
turns leaves scarlet.
Hush shakes the monkeypod
till pink petal-tongues fall.

You're home in New York.
I'm back here in Bogalusa
with one foot in pinewoods.
The mockingbird's blue note
sounds to me like *please*,

please. A beaten song
threaded through the skull
by cross hairs.
Black hands still turn blood red
working the strawberry fields.

The Thorn Merchant

There are teeth marks
on everything he loves.
When he enters the long room
more solemn than a threadbare Joseph coat,
the Minister of Hard Knocks & Golden Keys
begins to shuffle his feet.
The ink on contracts disappears.
Another stool pigeon leans
over a wrought-iron balcony.
Blood money's at work.
While men in black wetsuits
drag Blue Lake, his hands dally
at the hem of his daughter's skirt.

In the brain's shooting gallery
he goes down real slow.
His heart suspended in a mirror,
shadow of a crow over a lake.
With his fingers around his throat
he moans like a statue
of straw on a hillside.
Ready to auction off his hands
to the highest bidder,
he knows how death waits
in us like a light switch.

The Thorn Merchant's Right-Hand Man

Well, that's Pretty Boy Emeritus
alias Leo the Machine, great-grandson
of Eddie the Immune, a real ladies' man
in his handmade elevated Spanish shoes.
It's funny how he walks into town
with just a bouquet or violin
& lost faces reappear, eclipsed
by fedoras in bulletproof
limousines. A looted brain case
succumbs & a cage of prayers
sways in night air. Pretty Boy throws a kiss
to death, a paradoxical star in each eye. Naturally
he's surprised when he stumbles
& snags his suit coat on an ice pick.
It had to happen. He's caught
in a Texaco john humming the Mass in D.
The fight moves out to the corner
of Midsummer Avenue & Galante Blvd.
like two men tussling with red lanterns.
Pretty Boy's shoelaces tied together,
the full moon behind flowering manzanita
deserts him with his tongue in pawn
clear down to where a plea forms
the root word for flesh.

The Heart's Graveyard Shift

I lose faith in my left hand
not because my dog Echo's eloped
with ignis fatuus into pinewoods
or that my limp's unhealed
after 13 years. What can go wrong
goes wrong, & between loves an empty
space defines itself like a stone's weight
helps it to sink into earth.
My devil-may-care attitude
returns overnight, the bagwoman
outside the 42nd Street Automat
is now my muse. I should know
by heart the schema, routes
A & B, points where we
flip coins, heads or tails,
to stay alive. Between loves
I crave danger; the assassin's cross hairs
underline my point of view.

                      Between loves,
with a pinch of madness tucked under
the tongue, a man might fly off the handle
& kill his best friend over a penny.
His voice can break into butterflies
just as the eight ball cracks
across deep-green felt,
growing silent with something unsaid
like a mouth stuffed with nails.
He can go off his rocker, sell the family
business for a dollar, next morning
pull a Brink's job & hijack a 747.
He can hook up with a woman in silver
spike heels who carries a metallic blue guitar
or he can get right with Jesus
through phenobarbital.

                    Between loves
I sing all night with the jukebox:
"Every man's gotta cry for himself."
I play chicken with the Midnight Special

rounding Dead Man's Curve, enthralled
by the northern lights & machinery
of falling stars. Internal solstice,
my body, a poorly rigged by-pass
along Desperado Ave., taking me away
from myself. Equilibrium's whorehouses.
Arcades scattered along the eastern seaboard.
I search dead-colored shells for clues,
visions, for a thread of meat,
untelling interior landscapes.
A scarecrow dances away with my shadow.
Between loves I could stand all day
at a window watching honeysuckle open
as I make love to the ghosts
smuggled inside my head.

Boy Wearing a Dead Man's Clothes

1

I must say I never liked
garbardine's wornout shine.

Cold weather fills this coat,
& the shoulders have drooped anyhow!

Jesus, his yellow silk handkerchief;
I'm keeping this next to my heart.

The police chief's daughter's smile
has started to peel off

the curled photo I found
here in his breast pocket.

2

Blue denim cap, no other
crown for a poor man's head.

I wear it the same angle
he did, hipper than thou.

If I tilt it over my eyes,
a bit to the left this way,

cut the sky in half,
can I see the world

through his eyes? Cloud-cap
washed till there's hardly any blue left.

3

Uncle Jimmy's flowered shirt
keeps its shape. Body's character—

enamored of sweat, touch
gone out of the cloth,

no dark red map widening
across my chest to recall

that night.
Sleeves filled with silence.

The lipstick won't
come off.

4
I don't belong here. I
can't help but say

to Uncle's cordovan boots,
Get me outta East Texas, back to L.A.,

but please don't take me
by their place: Four weeks ago, that time

I saw him & Mrs. Overstreet
kissing in the doorway,

& Mr. Overstreet drunk
with his head on the table.

The Music That Hurts

Put away those insipid spoons.
The frontal lobe horn section went home hours ago.
The trap drum has been kicked
down the fire escape,
& the tenor's ballad amputated.
Inspiration packed her bags.
Her caftan recurs in the foggy doorway
like brain damage; the soft piano solo of her walk
evaporates; memory loses her exquisite tongue,
looking for "green silk stockings with gold seams"
on a nail over the bathroom mirror.
Tonight I sleep with Silence,
my impossible white wife.

When in Rome—Apologia

Please forgive me, sir,
for getting involved

in the music—
it's my innate weakness

for the cello: so human.
Please forgive me
for the attention

I've given your wife
tonight, sir.

I was taken in by her
strand of pearls,
enchanted by a piano
riff in the cortex,
by a secret

anticipation. I don't know
what came over me, sir.

After three Jack Daniel's
you must overlook
my candor, my lack of
sequitur.

I could talk
about Odysseus

& Athena, sexual
flowers, autogamy
or Nothingness.

I got carried away
by the swing of her hips.

But take no offense
if I return to the matter

as if hormonal.
I must confess
my love for black silk, sir.
I apologize for
the eyes in my head.

The Thorn Merchant's Wife

She meditates on how rocks rise
in Bluebird Canyon, how hills
tremble as she makes love
to herself, how memories drift
& nod like belladonna
kissing the ground.

She remembers the first time, there
in his flashy two-tone Buick.
That night she was a big smile
in the moon's broken-down alley.
When she became the Madonna of Closed Eyes
nightmares bandaged each other
with old alibis & surgical gauze,
that red dress he fell for
turned to ghost cloth
in some bagwoman's wardrobe.

She thinks about the gardener's son.
But those black-haired hours only lasted
till the shake dancer's daughter
got into his blood & he grew sober—
before solitaire began to steal
her nights, stringing an opus
of worry beads, before Morphine
leaned into the gold frame.

The Thorn Merchant's Mistress

I was on my high
horse then. I
wore red with ease

& I knew how
to walk. There
were men undressing me

everywhere I went,
& women wishing
themselves in my place,

a swan unfractured
by August. I was still
a girl. If they

wanted culture,
I said Vivaldi
& Plato's Cave.

If they wanted
the streets, I said
Fuck you.

I knew how
to plead, Wait, Wait,
till I caught the eye

of some *deus ex
machina*. I was in
a deep dance

pulling the hidden
strings of nude
shadows. But when

his car drove by
my heart caught
like a fat moth

in spider web. Goddamn!
I didn't know
how to say No.

After Summer Fell Apart

I can't touch you.
His face always returns;
we exchange long looks
in each bad dream
& what I see, my God.
Honey, sweetheart,
I hold you against me
but nothing works.
Two boats moored,
rocking between nowhere
& nowhere.
A bone inside me whispers
maybe tonight,
but I keep thinking
about the two men wrestling nude
in Lawrence's *Women in Love.*
I can't get past
reels of breath unwinding.
He has you. Now
he doesn't. He has you
again. Now he doesn't.

You're at the edge of azaleas
shaken loose by a word.
I see your rose-colored
skirt unfurl.
He has a knife
to your throat,
night birds come back
to their branches.
A hard wind raps at the door,
the new year prowling
in a black overcoat.
It's been six months
since we made love.
Tonight I look at you
hugging the pillow,
half smiling in your sleep.
I want to shake you & ask
who. Again I touch myself,

unashamed, until
his face comes into focus.
He's stolen something
from me & I don't know
if it has a name or not—
like counting your ribs
with one foolish hand
& mine with the other.

The Brain to the Heart

Stars tied to breath
don't have to be there
when you look.
No more than drops
of blood on ginkgo
leaves & inconsequential

eggs & frog spittle
clinging to damp grass.
Sure, I've seen doubts
clustered like peacock
eyes flash green fire.
So what?

When days are strung together,
the hourglass fills
with worm's dirt.
What do you take
the brain for? I know
how hard you work

in that dark place, but
I can't be tied down
to shadows of men
in trenches you won't
forget. You look at
a mulberry leaf

like a silkworm does, with all your insides,
but please don't ask me to be responsible.

Audacity of the Lower Gods

I know salt marshes that move along like one big
trembling wing. I've noticed insects
shiny as gold in a blues singer's teeth
& more keenly calibrated than a railroad watch,
but at heart I'm another breed.

The audacity of the lower gods—
whatever we name we own.
Diversiloba, we say, unfolding poison oak.
Lovers go untouched as we lean from bay windows
with telescopes trained on a yellow sky.

I'd rather let the flowers
keep doing what they do best.
Unblessing each petal,
letting go a year's worth of white
death notes, busily unnaming themselves.

The Falling-Down Song

Here I am
with one foot on a floating platform
breaking myself into small defeats—
I'm the ghost of a moneychanger
& halo of flies, half-moon of false teeth
unable to bite bread. Please
go, & tell no one you've seen me under the cypress,
a fool-hearted footstool,
termites in my two
sad wooden
legs,
sawdust in my black leather shoes.

The Thorn Merchant's Son

Using an old water-stained
Seven Year Itch movie poster
as his dartboard, he places
all six into the bull's-eye.
The phonograph clicks silently,
playing "Teen Angel" the tenth time.
Sipping a Pepsi-Cola,
he moves over to *Pretty Baby*
unrolled on his daddy's desk.
He runs his tongue around
the edge of her smile,
then picks up a paperweight
& shakes it till the black horse
disappears inside the glass.
Grey-eyed opacity, low cloud
coming over the room, he throws
a wooden puzzle against a wall
& the fist-shaped piece
flies apart like a clay pigeon.
He stares fifteen minutes
at a tintype face
so blue it's hardly there.
With a little dance step
he eases over & props an elbow
on the window sill, aiming
his high-powered binoculars
at a woman's bedroom window.

I Apologize

My mind wasn't even there.
Mirage, sir. I didn't see
what I thought I saw.
Que será, será. That's that.
I was in my woman's bedroom
removing her red shoes & dress.
I'm just like the rest of the world:
No comment; no way, Jose;
I want spring always
dancing with the pepper trees.
I was miles away, I saw nothing!
Did I say their diamond rings
blinded me & I nearly lost my head?
I think it was how the North
Star fell through plate glass.
I don't remember what they wore.
What if I said they were
only shadows of overcoats
stooped in the doorway
where the light's bad?
No, no one roughed me up last night.
Sir, there's no story to change.
I heard no names. There were no
distinguishing marks or other clues.
No slip of the tongue. This morning
I can't even remember who I am.

1984

The year burns an icon
into the blood. Birdlime
discolors the glass domes
& roof beams grow shaky as old men
in the lobby of Heartbreak Hotel.
Purple oxide gas lamps light
the way out of this paradise.
We laugh behind masks & lip-sync Cobol.
We're transmitters for pigeons
with microphones in their heads.
Yellow sky over stockyards,
& by the grace of God
rockets hum in white silos
buried in Kansas wheat fields
or nailed to some ragged hill
zoned as a perfect fearscape.

We say, "I've seen it all."
Bombardment & psychic flux,
not just art nouveau tabula rasa
or double helix. We're ancient mariners
counting wishbones, in supersonic hulls
humming the falconer's ditty
over a banged-up job.
Three Mile Island blooms
her dreamworld as we wait
on the edge of our chairs
for the drunk radiologist.
Such a lovely view—
Big Brother to shadows
slipping under the door
where the millstones are stored.

We sing the ghost-catcher's madrigal.
The end of what? To count dismembered years
we say Gandhi, JFK, King,
leafing through names & faces. Waves
of locusts fall like black snow
in our sleep. Grackles
foresee ruins & battlements

where the Bone Breakers & God Squad
have had a good old time—
destined to sleep under
swaying trestles, as yes-men
crowded into a bad season,
listening all night to a calliope
hoot the equinox.

Since our hair's standing up
on the backs of our necks,
we must be on to something good,
Oppenheimer, right? Killjoy's
perched like Khan of the Golden Horde
on the back of a prisoner,
& we sit eating crow,
picking teeth with gold toothpicks.
Angels playing with trick mirrors,
sweet on a Minotaur in the dark
muscular air of a penny arcade.
We can transplant broken hearts
but can we put goodness back into them?

Brass knuckles flash
& this year is like flesh
torn under a lover's eye.
The end of what?
Going after posthumous love letters
dumped in black holes
light-years away, we line up
for practice runs with portable
neutron bombs strapped
to our backs—lopsided fun houses
where everyone wants to be
king of the stacked deck.

Streamlined androids construct
replicas three thousand miles away.
We guardians of uglier things to come
with our camera obscuras,
light vigil candles
& work the White Angel
bread line. Following the lunar crab

& loving the skyline, we discover
there's nothing to hold down tombstones,
lovers wishing upon astronauts
flashier than rock stars.

Alloyed against common sense,
somehow we're all King Lears
calling forth kingdom come—
scherzo for brimstone.
Fireworks bring in the New Year
& Zeus the confused robot
punches a fist through a skylight
as he dances across the floor
with his mechanical bride
doing a bionic two-step.

Hammered silver,
those badges we wear:
U-235 UTOPIA.
Made in America.
"Give us enough time,
we'll make the damn thing.
Let's look at the manual.
OK, here's *human breath*
on page 319."

Weather wars hang in skies
over the Third World. The dead
keep walking toward the sea
with everything they own
on their backs. Caught off guard
our falsehoods break into parts
of speech, like mayflies
on windshields of white Corvettes.

We're stargazers, weirdos,
prestidigitators in bluesy
bedrooms, on private trips
to the moon. The end of what?
We lock our hearts
into idle, not sure
of this world or the next.

Let's come down to earth.
Let's forget those video wrist watches
& "E.T." dolls triggered
by interstellar sundials
where electric eyes
hum on 18-carat key chains

& Dr. Strangelove tracks
the titanium gods. Let's go
beyond Devil's Triangle,
back to where the heart knows.
All the machines are on.
We sleepwalk among black roses
like characters in a dime novel,
& psychotherapy
can't erase the sign of the beast.

Dreambook Bestiary

Fear's Understudy

Like some lost part of a model kit
for Sir Dogma's cracked armor
an armadillo merges with night.
It rests against a mossy stone.
A steel-gray safe-deposit box,
ground level, two quicksilver eyes
peer out from under a coral helmet
color of fossil. It lives
encased in an asbestos hull
at the edge of a kingdom
of blackberries in quagmire,
in a grassy daydream,
sucked into its shield
by logic of flesh.

The Art of Atrophy

The possum plays dead
as Spanish moss, a seasoned actor
giving us his dumb show.
He dreams of ripe persimmons,
watching a dried stick
beside a white thunderstone,
with one eye half-open, a grin
slipping from the crooked corners
of his mouth, that old silver moon
playing tricks again. How long
can he play this waiting game,
till the season collapses,
till blowflies, worms, & ants
crawl into his dull coat
& sneak him away under
the evening star? Now
he's a master escape artist
like Lazarus, the gray
lining from a workman's glove
lost in frost-colored leaves.

Heart of the Rose Garden

A cluster of microscopic mouths
all working at once—

ants improve the soil, sift dust
through a millennium of wings.

They subsist on fear, drawn
to the lovebone,

to the base of the skull
where a slow undermining takes shape.

Under moonlight they begin their
instinctual autopsy, sensing

when grief tracks
someone down in her red patent-leather shoes,

when a man's soul
slips behind a headstone.

Glimpse
Near a spidery cage of grass
this cripple inches sideways up a sandy trail
with its little confiscated burden.
Just bigger than a man's thumbnail,
light as the shadow of a bone.

The sea falls short again. Claws unfold.
Its body almost creeps out. Morning
ticks away. Playing yes, no,
maybe so, it places its dome-shack
down on the sand & backs off,
surveying for the first tremor of loss.

Underside of Light
Centipede. Tubular, bright egg sac
trailing like a lodestone (unable to say
which is dragging which) out of damp compost:
biological soil, miasma, where lightning
starts like a sharp pain in god's spine.

In its armor, this sentinel rises
from a vault of double blackness.
This vegetal love forecasting April
crawls toward murdering light,
first thing tied to last.

Jonestown: More Eyes for *Jadwiga's Dream*

After Rousseau

Brighter than crisp new money.
Birds unfold wings into nervous fans,
adrift like breath-drawn kites, among
tremulous fronds with flowers crimson
as muzzle flash. Tropic silk, root color,
ocean green, they float to tree limbs
like weary scarves.

Hidden eyes deepen the memory
between sunrise & nightmare. Pine-box builders
grin with the pale soothsayer presiding over
this end of songs. The day's a thick hive
of foliage, not the moss grief deposits
on damp stones—we're unable to tell where
fiction bleeds into the real.

Some unspoken voice, small as a lizard's,
is trying to obey the trees.
Green birds flare up behind church bells
against the heartscape: if only
they'd fold their crepe-paper wings
over bruised eyes & see nothing
but night in their brains.

Landscape for the Disappeared

Lo & behold. Yes, peat bogs
in Louisiana. The dead
stumble home like swamp fog,
our lost uncles & granddaddies
come back to us almost healed.
Knob-fingered & splayfooted,
all the has-been men
& women rise through nighttime
into our slow useless days.

Live oak & cypress
counting these shapes in a dance
human forms aren't made for. Faces
waterlogged into their own
pure expression, unanswerable
questions on their lips.

Dumbstruck premonitions rise
from the heckle-grass
to search us out.
Guilty, sings the screech owl.
I hear the hair keeps growing
in the grave. Here
moss lets down a damp light.

We call back the ones
we've never known, with stories
more ours than theirs.
The wind's low cry
their language, a lunar rainbow
lost among Venus's-flytraps
yellowing in frog spittle & downward mire,
boatloads of contraband
guns & slot machines dumped
through the years.

Here's this lovely face so black
with marsh salt. Her smile,
a place where minnows swim.
All the full presence
shiny as a skull under the skin.
Say it again—we are
spared nothing.

Good Joe

We prop him up
in his easy chair.
We give him a crew cut.
We dust off his blue serge.
We sing his favorite
golden oldies: "Dixie"
& "Ta-ra-ra-boom-de-ay!"
We clamp on his false
finger bones. We lead him
across the floor
saying, "Walk, walk."
We move in circles
dancing the McCarthy—
someone leans over & clicks in
his glass eye. All his ideas
come into focus;
we hear rats in the walls
multiplying.

Professors, photojournalists,
scholars of ashes in urns
buried a thousand years
off the Gulf of Mexico
sign loyalty oaths; actors
forget their meaty lines.
We shine his wing-tip Bostonians.
We bring him oyster stew,
bottles of Chivas Regal
on a jade serving tray.
We show him snapshots of lovers.
We give him a book of names,
turning the pages for him.
Some of us volunteer
to enter a room

where machines take each other apart
& put themselves back
together. We form
a line which spills out
the door, around the corner
for a whole city block,
& with bowed heads
pay protection.

In the Background of Silence

First, worms begin with a man's mind.
Then they eat away his left shoe
to answer his final question.
His heart turns into a gold thimble of ashes,
his bones remind bees of honeycomb,
he falls back into himself like dirt into a hole,
his soul fits into a matchbox
in the shirt pocket
of his brother's well-tailored uniform.

Not even a stray dog dares to stir in the plaza,
after the muzzle flash,
after black coffee & Benzedrine,
after the sign of the cross a hundred times,
after sorrow's skirt drops to the floor,
after the soldier pulls off his spit-shined boots
& crawls into bed with the prettiest woman in town.

For the Walking Dead

Veronica passes her cape between breath
& death, rehearsing
the body's old rhyme.
With boyish soldiers on their way
to the front, she dances
the slowdrag in a bar called
Pylos. White phosphorus blooms
five miles away, burning sky
for a long moment, mortars
rock in iron shoes cradled
by earth, within earshot
of carbines stuttering through
elephant grass. Canisters lobbed
over night hills whine
like moonstruck dogs. After-
silence falls into the valley.

Tunes on the outdated jukebox
take her back to St. Louis,
back to where the color of her eyes
served as no one's balsam.
"Please," they whisper in her ear
as she counts the unreturned
faces, pale beads on an abacus.
Skin-colored dawn unravels
& a gun turret pivots on a hill.
Amputated ghosts on the walls—
she pulls them to her,
knowing the bruise beforehand.
She lets them work her into
the bar's darkest corner.
They hold her, a shield
against everything they know.

Child's Play

Hair slicked back as if
he just eased up out of
womb-water, the young man
wears a fatigue jacket.
The shoulder patch says
Seven Steps to Hell.
Dancing with the machine,
he tries to coax Thundarr
up from the black box
deep in the belly of metal.
The Cosmic Death's-Head
wars with Captain Sky.
A woman in punk-rocker black
plays Asteroids, leaning
her shadow against his
on the bus-terminal wall.
His hands work with chrome,
rockets zoom across the screen
silent as a sperm count.
His knuckles grow white
gripping the knobs,
with his collar turned up
like John Travolta's.
He gazes down in the glass
aiming for a clean kill,
not nearly as dangerous
as he wants you to think.

The Beast & Burden: Seven Improvisations

      1   The Vicious
Fear threads its song
through the bones.
Syringe, stylus,
or pearl-handled stiletto?
He's fallen in love
with the Spanish garrote;
trailing a blue feather over the beast's belly
on down between his toes.
Night-long laughter
leaks from under the sheet-metal door.

Blackout.

———

He sits under a floodlight
mumbling that a theory of ants
will finally deal with us,

& reading My Lord Rochester
to a golden sky over Johannesburg,
a stray dog beside him, Sirius
licking his combat boots.

      2   The Decadent
Herr Scalawag, Esq.
dances the come-on
in Miss Misery's
spike heels.
He does a hellcat
high step stolen
from Josephine Baker,
holding a fake flower
like a flimsy excuse.
A paper rose, poppy
odor of luck
& lust. Look,
he's placed himself
upon the night's maddening wheel,
reduced from flesh

into the stuff
dreams are made of.
                    Hum-job,
his smile working
like a time-released
Mickey Finn.

        3   *The Esoteric*
Unable to move the muse with narcotic
sweet talk, he muscles in on someone's grief.

He's on the glassy edge
of his stepping stone, a ghost
puppet stealing light from the real
world. With a wild guess
for spine, a face half-finished
on the blind lithographer's desk.

Canticle, cleftsong & heartriff
stolen out of another's mouth,
effigy's prologue & bravado.
He fingers his heirloom
Bible with rows of exed out names
& dried roses between yellow pages,

searching for an idiom
based on the color of his eyes.

        4   *The Sanctimonious*
She wakes to find herself washing
the beast's wounds.
The Woman at the Well
with bare feet in compost,
emissary to the broken. She leans

her body against this born loser,
her hip into his ungodly mercy,
her hair sways with his breathing,
her mind intent on an hourglass
on a stone shelf. Bronze green.

By now, as they rock
in each other's embrace
in the cold half-light,

she knows every doubtful wish
inside his housebroken head.

          5   *The Vindictive*
Smiley, the jailer
hums the bowstring's litany.
His pale voice breaks
into a bittersweetness,
his face no more
than a half-page
profile from a wanted poster.
The iron door eases open.
Blameful mask, memory's
notorious white glove
unstitches the heartstring.
His leaden stare tabulates
the spinal column like a throw
of the dice. Satisfied
defeat has taken root,
he smiles down at the prisoner
on the cell floor, his touch
burning like candlelight & crab lice
through black hair. Wagner's
Ring of the Nibelung
plays on radio across the corridor
& the smell of mignonette
comes through the bars. He
tightens his mystical sleephold—
a carbuncle of joy
underneath his kiss.

          6   *Exorcism*
The beast's charisma
unravels the way a smoke flower
turns into dust. Hugging
the shadow of a broken wing
beauty & ugliness conspire.
Forced to use his weight perfectly
against himself, the beast is
transmogrified into the burden
& locked in wooden stocks
braced by a cross to bear.
O how geranium-scented melancholia
works on the body—

smell of ether, gut string
trailing lost memories.
Detached from whatever remains,
one note of bliss still burns his tongue.

7   *Epilogue: Communion*

The beast & the burden lock-step waltz. Tiger lily &
screwworm, it all adds up to this: bloodstar & molecular
burning kiss. Conception. The grooved sockets slip into
each other, sinking into pain, a little deeper into earth's
habit. Tongue in juice meat, uncertain conversion, cock
& heart entangled, ragweed in bloom. A single sigh of
glory, the two put an armlock on each other—matched
for strength, leg over leg. Double bind & slow dance on
ball-bearing feet. Arm in arm & slipknot. Birth, death,
back to back—silent mouth against the other's ear. They
sing a duet: *e pluribus unum*. The spirit hinged to a
single tree. No deeper color stolen from midnight sky—
they're in the same shape, as meat collects around a
bone, almost immortal, like a centaur's future perfect
dream.

Neon
Vernacular

from *Toys in a Field*

Ambush

So quiet birds
start singing again.
Lizards bring a touch of light.
The squad leader counts bullets
a third time. Stars
glint off gunbarrels.
We can almost hear a leaf
falling. "For chrissake. Please."
Raw opium intoxicates
a blaze of insects.
Buddhist monks on a hill
burn twelve red lanterns.
"Put out your stupid cigarette,
PFC," the Recon corporal whispers.
The trees play games.
A tiger circles us, in his broken cage
between sky & what's human.
"We'll wait out the bastards.
They have to come this way,
& when they do, not
even God can help 'em."
Headless shadows skirt the hedgerow.
A crossroad for lost birds
singing their hearts out
calling to the dead,
& then a sound that makes you jump
in your sleep years later,
the cough of a mortar tube.

Monsoon Season

A river shines in the jungle's
wet leaves. The rain's finally
let up but whenever wind shakes
the foliage it starts to fall.
The monsoon uncovers troubled
seasons we tried to forget.
Dead men slip through bad weather,
stamping their muddy boots to wake us,
their curses coming easier.
There's a bend in everything,
in elephant grass & flame trees,
raindrops pelting the sand-bagged
bunker like a muted gong.
White phosphorus washed from the air,
wind sways with violet myrtle,
beating it naked. Soaked to the bone,
jungle rot brings us down to earth.
We sit in our hooches
with too much time,
where grounded choppers
can't fly out the wounded.
Somewhere nearby a frog
begs a snake.
I try counting droplets,
stars that aren't in the sky.
My poncho feels like a body bag.
I lose count. Red leaves
whirl by, the monsoon
unburying the dead.

Water Buffalo

God, this mud. Fear's habit.
This red-caped dusk.
The iron bird rattles
overhead again, with stars
falling, the green man
strapped in its smoky doorhole.
I drop my head & charge
a vulture's shadow gliding
over a rice paddy dike.
Hung belly, hooves, & asshole,
everything pushes against my eyes.
I bellow at the sunset
like a brass foghorn.
Shooting up, away from my holler,
sparrows eclipse. Sunday's
whole weight rests on my back.
The whirlwind machine
returns, hammering its gong.
I'm nothing but a target.
It nose-dives.
I plant my feet, big as myth,
& hear silent applause.
The earth pulls at me
& the day caves in.
Silver lances ignite the air.
Bullheaded dynamo—I'm
no match for that fire,
for what's in a heart.

Le Xuan, Beautiful Spring

I run my fingers over a photo
torn from a magazine & folded
inside *Sons and Lovers*.
She's got one hand on her hip
& the other aiming a revolver
at some target hiding
from the camera. Flanked by a cadre
of women in fatigues, she's daring
the sun to penetrate her *ao dai*.
High-ranking officers let their eyes
travel over silk as they push pins
into maps under a dead-looking sky.

Shadows crawl from under her feet.
Does she know soldiers undress her
behind dark aviation glasses?
She's delicate as a reed
against a river, just weighing the gun
in her hand, a blood-tipped lotus
rooted in the torn air.
Another kind of lust blooms
in flesh, ominous as a photo
on a coffin waiting to be
lost among papers & notes,
but it still hurts when a pistol
plays with the heart this way.

Please

Forgive me, soldier.
    Forgive my right hand
                for pointing you
            to the flawless
tree line now
    outlined in my brain.
          There was so much
bloodsky over our heads at daybreak
         in Pleiku, but I won't say
        those infernal guns
        blinded me on that hill.

Mistakes piled up men like clouds
    pushed to the dark side.
      Sometimes I try to retrace
        them, running
          my fingers down the map
            telling less than a woman's body—
we followed the grid coordinates
    in some battalion commander's mind.
        If I could make my mouth
          unsay those orders,
          I'd holler: Don't
            move a muscle.
             Stay put,
& keep your fucking head
down, soldier.

Ambush.
Gutsmoke.
    Last night
      while making love
          I cried out,
          Hit the dirt!
            I've tried to swallow my tongue.
      You were a greenhorn, so fearless,
even foolish, & when I said *go*, Henry,
         you went dancing on a red string
of bullets from that tree line
as it moved from a low cloud.

Neon Vernacular

from *Dien Cai Dau*

Camouflaging the Chimera

We tied branches to our helmets.
We painted our faces & rifles
with mud from a riverbank,

blades of grass hung from the pockets
of our tiger suits. We wove
ourselves into the terrain,
content to be a hummingbird's target.

We hugged bamboo & leaned
against a breeze off the river,
slow-dragging with ghosts

from Saigon to Bangkok,
with women left in doorways
reaching in from America.
We aimed at dark-hearted songbirds.

In our way station of shadows
rock apes tried to blow our cover,
throwing stones at the sunset. Chameleons

crawled our spines, changing from day
to night: green to gold,
gold to black. But we waited
till the moon touched metal,

till something almost broke
inside us. VC struggled
with the hillside, like black silk

wrestling iron through grass.
We weren't there. The river ran
through our bones. Small animals took refuge
against our bodies; we held our breath,

ready to spring the L-shaped
ambush, as a world revolved
under each man's eyelid.

Tunnels

Crawling down headfirst into the hole,
he kicks the air & disappears.
I feel like I'm down there
with him, moving ahead, pushed
by a river of darkness, feeling
blessed for each inch of the unknown.
Our tunnel rat is the smallest man
in the platoon, in an echo chamber
that makes his ears bleed
when he pulls the trigger.
He moves as if trying to outdo
blind fish easing toward imagined blue,
pulled by something greater than life's
ambitions. He can't think about
spiders & scorpions mending the air,
or care about bats upside down
like gods in the mole's blackness.
The damp smell goes deeper
than the stench of honey buckets.
A web of booby traps waits, ready
to spring into broken stars.
Forced onward by some need,
some urge, he knows the pulse
of mysteries & diversions
like thoughts trapped in the ground.
He questions each root.
Every cornered shadow has a life
to bargain with. Like an angel
pushed up against what hurts,
his globe-shaped helmet
follows the gold ring his flashlight
casts into the void. Through silver
lice, shit, maggots, & vapor of pestilence,
he goes, the good soldier,
on hands & knees, tunneling past
death sacked into a blind corner,
loving the weight of the shotgun
that will someday dig his grave.

Starlight Scope Myopia

Gray-blue shadows lift
shadows onto an oxcart.

Making night work for us,
the starlight scope brings
men into killing range.

The river under Vi Bridge
takes the heart away

like the Water God
riding his dragon.
Smoke-colored

Viet Cong
move under our eyelids,

lords over loneliness
winding like coral vine through
sandalwood & lotus,

inside our lowered heads
years after this scene

ends. The brain closes
down. What looks like
one step into the trees,

they're lifting crates of ammo
& sacks of rice, swaying

under their shared weight.
Caught in the infrared,
what are they saying?

Are they talking about women
or calling the Americans

beaucoup dien cai dau?
One of them is laughing.
You want to place a finger

to his lips & say "shhhh."
You try reading ghost talk

on their lips. They say
"up-up we go," lifting as one.
This one, old, bowlegged,

you feel you could reach out
& take him into your arms. You

peer down the sights of your M-16,
seeing the full moon
loaded on an oxcart.

Hanoi Hannah

Ray Charles! His voice
calls from waist-high grass,
& we duck behind gray sandbags.
"Hello, Soul Brothers. Yeah,
Georgia's also on my mind."
Flares bloom over the trees.
"Here's Hannah again.
Let's see if we can't
light her goddamn fuse
this time." Artillery
shells carve a white arc
against dusk. Her voice rises
from a hedgerow on our left.
"It's Saturday night in the States.
Guess what your woman's doing tonight.
I think I'll let Tina Turner
tell you, you homesick GIs."
Howitzers buck like a herd
of horses behind concertina.
"You know you're dead men,
don't you? You're dead
as King today in Memphis.
Boys, you're surrounded by
General Tran Do's division."
Her knife-edge song cuts
deep as a sniper's bullet.
"Soul Brothers, what you dying for?"
We lay down a white-klieg
trail of tracers. Phantom jets
fan out over the trees.
Artillery fire zeros in.
Her voice grows flesh
& we can see her falling
into words, a bleeding flower
no one knows the true name for.
"You're lousy shots, GIs."
Her laughter floats up
as though the airways are
buried under our feet.

"You and I Are Disappearing"

—Björn Håkansson

The cry I bring down from the hills
belongs to a girl still burning
inside my head. At daybreak
    she burns like a piece of paper.
She burns like foxfire
in a thigh-shaped valley.
A skirt of flames
dances around her
at dusk.
      We stand with our hands
hanging at our sides,
while she burns
    like a sack of dry ice.
She burns like oil on water.
She burns like a cattail torch
dipped in gasoline.
She glows like the fat tip
of a banker's cigar,
    silent as quicksilver.
A tiger under a rainbow
  at nightfall.
She burns like a shot glass of vodka.
She burns like a field of poppies
at the edge of a rain forest.
She rises like dragonsmoke
    to my nostrils.
She burns like a burning bush
driven by a godawful wind.

Re-creating the Scene

The metal door groans
& folds shut like an ancient turtle
that won't let go
of a finger till it thunders.
The Confederate flag
flaps from a radio antenna,
& the woman's clothes
come apart in their hands.
Their mouths find hers
in the titanic darkness
of the steel grotto,
as she counts the names of dead
ancestors, shielding a baby
in her arms. The three men
ride her breath, grunting
over lovers back in Mississippi.
She floats on their rage
like a torn water flower,
defining night inside a machine
where men are gods.
The season quietly sweats.
They hold her down
with their eyes,
taking turns, piling stones
on her father's grave.
The APC rolls with curves of the land,
up hills & down into gullies,
crushing trees & grass,
droning like a constellation
of locusts eating through bamboo,
creating the motion for their bodies.

She rises from the dust
& pulls the torn garment
around her, staring after the APC
till it's small enough
to fit like a toy tank in her hands.
She turns in a circle,
pounding the samarium dust
with her feet where the steel

tracks have plowed. The sun
fizzes like a pill in a glass
of water, & for a moment
the world's future tense:
She approaches the MPs
at the gate; a captain from G-5
accosts her with candy kisses;
I inform *The Overseas Weekly*;
flashbulbs refract her face
in a room of polished brass
& spit-shined boots;
on the trial's second day
she turns into mist—
someone says money
changed hands,
& someone else swears
she's buried at LZ Gator.
But for now, the baby
makes a fist & grabs at the air,
searching for a breast.

We Never Know

He danced with tall grass
for a moment, like he was swaying
with a woman. Our gun barrels
glowed white-hot.
When I got to him,
a blue halo
of flies had already claimed him.
I pulled the crumbled photograph
from his fingers.
There's no other way
to say this: I fell in love.
The morning cleared again,
except for a distant mortar
& somewhere choppers taking off.
I slid the wallet into his pocket
& turned him over, so he wouldn't be
kissing the ground.

A Break from the Bush

The South China Sea
drives in another herd.
The volleyball's a punching bag:
Clem's already lost a tooth
& Johnny's left eye is swollen shut.
Frozen airlifted steaks burn
on a wire grill, & miles away
machine guns can be heard.
Pretending we're somewhere else,
we play harder.
Lee Otis, the point man,
high on Buddha grass,
buries himself up to his neck
in sand. "Can you see me now?
In this spot they gonna build
a Hilton. Invest in Paradise.
Bang, bozos! You're dead."
Frenchie's cassette player
unravels Hendrix's "Purple Haze."
Snake, 17, from Daytona,
sits at the water's edge,
the ash on his cigarette
pointing to the ground
like a crooked finger. CJ,
who in three days will trip
a fragmentation mine,
runs after the ball
into the whitecaps,
laughing.

Tu Do Street

Music divides the evening.
I close my eyes & can see
men drawing lines in the dust.
America pushes through the membrane
of mist & smoke, & I'm a small boy
again in Bogalusa. *White Only*
signs & Hank Snow. But tonight
I walk into a place where bar girls
fade like tropical birds. When
I order a beer, the mama-san
behind the counter acts as if she
can't understand, while her eyes
skirt each white face, as Hank Williams
calls from the psychedelic jukebox.
We have played Judas where
only machine-gun fire brings us
together. Down the street
black GIs hold to their turf also.
An off-limits sign pulls me
deeper into alleys, as I look
for a softness behind these voices
wounded by their beauty & war.
Back in the bush at Dak To
& Khe Sanh, we fought
the brothers of these women
we now run to hold in our arms.
There's more than a nation
inside us, as black & white
soldiers touch the same lovers
minutes apart, tasting
each other's breath,
without knowing these rooms
run into each other like tunnels
leading to the underworld.

Communiqué

Bob Hope's on stage, but we want the Gold Diggers,
want a flash of legs

through the hemorrhage of vermilion, giving us
something to kill for.

We want our hearts wrung out like rags & ground down
to Georgia dust

while Cobras drag the perimeter, gliding along the sea,
swinging searchlights

through the trees. The assault & battery of hot pink
glitter erupts

as the rock 'n' roll band tears down the night—caught
in a safety net

of brightness, The Gold Diggers convulse. White legs
shimmer like strobes.

The lead guitarist's right foot's welded to his wah-wah.
"I thought you said

Aretha was gonna be here." "Man, I don't wanna see
no Miss America."

"There's Lola." The sky is blurred by magnesium flares
over the fishing boats.

"Shit, man, she looks awful white to me." We duck
when we hear the quick

metallic hiss of the mountain of amplifiers struck by
a flash of rain.

After the show's packed up & gone, after the choppers
have flown out backwards,

after the music & colors have died slowly in our heads,
& the downpour's picked up,

we sit holding our helmets like rain-polished skulls.

Prisoners

Usually at the helipad
I see them stumble-dance
across the hot asphalt
with crokersacks over their heads,
moving toward the interrogation huts,
thin-framed as box kites
of sticks & black silk
anticipating a hard wind
that'll tug & snatch them
out into space. I think
some must be laughing
under their dust-colored hoods,
knowing rockets are aimed
at Chu Lai—that the water's
evaporating & soon the nail
will make contact with metal.
How can anyone anywhere love
these half-broken figures
bent under the sky's brightness?
The weight they carry
is the soil we tread night & day.
Who can cry for them?
I've heard the old ones
are the hardest to break.
An arm twist, a combat boot
against the skull, a .45
jabbed into the mouth, nothing
works. When they start talking
with ancestors faint as camphor
smoke in pagodas, you know
you'll have to kill them
to get an answer.
Sunlight throws
scythes against the afternoon.
Everything's a heat mirage; a river
tugs at their slow feet.
I stand alone & amazed,
with a pill-happy door gunner
signaling for me to board the Cobra.
I remember how one day

I almost bowed to such figures
walking toward me, under
a corporal's ironclad stare.
I can't say why.
From a half-mile away
trees huddle together,
& the prisoners look like
marionettes hooked to strings of light.

Jungle Surrender

after Don Cooper's painting

Ghosts share us with the past & future
but we struggle to hold on to each breath.

Moving toward what waits behind the trees,
the prisoner goes deeper into himself, away

from how a man's heart divides him, deeper
into the jungle's indigo mystery & beauty,

with both hands raised into the air, only
surrendering halfway: the small man inside

waits like a photo in a shirt pocket, refusing
to raise his hands, silent & uncompromising

as the black scout dog beside him. Love & hate
flesh out the real man, how he wrestles

himself through a hallucination of blues
& deep purples that set the day on fire.

He sleepwalks a labyrinth of violet,
measuring footsteps from one tree to the next,

knowing we're all somehow connected.
What would I have said?

The real interrogator is a voice within.
I would have told them about my daughter

in Phoenix, how young she was,
about my first woman, anything

but how I helped ambush two Viet Cong
while plugged into the Grateful Dead.

For some, a soft windy voice makes them
snap. Blues & purples. Some place between

central Georgia & Tay Ninh Province—
the vision a knot of blood unravels

& parts of us we dared put into the picture
come together; the prisoner goes away

almost whole. But he will always touch
fraying edges of things, to feel hope break

like the worm that rejoins itself
under the soil . . . head to tail.

Thanks

Thanks for the tree
between me & a sniper's bullet.
I don't know what made the grass
sway seconds before the Viet Cong
raised his soundless rifle.
Some voice always followed,
telling me which foot
to put down first.
Thanks for deflecting the ricochet
against that anarchy of dusk.
I was back in San Francisco
wrapped up in a woman's wild colors,
causing some dark bird's love call
to be shattered by daylight
when my hands reached up
& pulled a branch away
from my face. Thanks
for the vague white flower
that pointed to the gleaming metal
reflecting how it is to be broken
like mist over the grass,
as we played some deadly
game for blind gods.
What made me spot the monarch
writhing on a single thread
tied to a farmer's gate,
holding the day together
like an unfingered guitar string,
is beyond me. Maybe the hills
grew weary & leaned a little in the heat.
Again, thanks for the dud
hand grenade tossed at my feet
outside Chu Lai. I'm still
falling through its silence.
I don't know why the intrepid
sun touched the bayonet,
but I know that something
stood among those lost trees
& moved only when I moved.

To Have Danced with Death

The black sergeant first class
who stalled us on the ramp
didn't kiss the ground either.

When two hearses sheened up to the plane
& government silver-gray coffins
rolled out on silent chrome coasters,

did he feel better? The empty left leg
of his trousers shivered as another hearse
with shiny hubcaps inched from behind a building . . .

his three rows of ribbons rainbowed
over the forest of faces through
plate glass. Afternoon sunlight

made surgical knives out of chrome
& brass. He half smiled when
the double doors opened for him

like a wordless mouth taking back promises.
The room of blue eyes averted his.
He stood there, searching

his pockets for something:
maybe a woman's name & number
worn thin as a Chinese fortune.

I wanted him to walk ahead,
to disappear through glass,
to be consumed by music

that might move him like Sandman Sims,
but he merely rocked on his good leg
like a bleak & soundless bell.

Report from the Skull's Diorama

Dr. King's photograph
comes at me from *White Nights*
like Hoover's imagination at work,

dissolving into a scenario
at Firebase San Juan Hill:
our chopper glides in closer,
down to the platoon of black GIs
back from night patrol

with five dead. Down
into a gold whirl of leaves
dust-deviling the fire base.
A field of black trees
stakes down the morning sun.

With the chopper blades
knife-fighting the air,
yellow leaflets quiver
back to the ground, clinging to us.
These men have lost their tongues,

but the red-bordered
leaflets tell us
VC didn't kill
Dr. Martin Luther King.
The silence etched into their skin

is also mine. Psychological
warfare colors the napalmed hill
gold-yellow. When our gunship
flies out backwards, rising
above the men left below

to blend in with the charred
landscape, an AK-47
speaks, with the leaflets
clinging to the men & stumps,
waving to me across the years.

Boat People

After midnight they load up.
A hundred shadows move about blindly.
Something close to sleep
hides low voices drifting
toward a red horizon. Tonight's
a black string, the moon's pull—
this boat's headed somewhere.
Lucky to have gotten past
searchlights low-crawling the sea,
like a woman shaking water
from her long dark hair.

Twelve times in three days
they've been lucky,
clinging to each other in gray mist.
Now Thai fishermen gaze out across
the sea as it changes color,
hands shading their eyes
the way sailors do,
minds on robbery & rape.
Sunlight burns blood-orange.

Storm warnings crackle on a radio.
The Thai fishermen turn away.
Not enough water for the trip.
The boat people cling to each other,
faces like yellow sea grapes,
wounded by doubt & salt.
Dusk hangs over the water.
Seasick, they daydream Jade Mountain
a whole world away, half-drunk
on what they hunger to become.

Missing in Action

Men start digging in the ground,
propping shadows against trees
outside Hanoi, but there aren't
enough bones for a hash pipe.
After they carve new names
into polished black stone,
we throw dust to the wind
& turn faces to blank walls.

Names we sing in sleep & anger
cling to willows like river mist.
We splice voices on tapes
but we can't make one man
walk the earth again.
Not a single song comes alive
in the ring of broken teeth
on the ground. Sunlight
presses down for an answer.
But nothing can make that C-130
over Hanoi come out of its spin,
spiraling like a flare in green sky.

After the flag's folded,
the living fall
into each other's arms.
They've left spaces
trees can't completely fill.
Pumping breath down tunnels
won't help us bring ghosts
across the sea.

Peasants outside Pakse City
insist the wildflowers
have changed colors.

They're what the wind
& rain have taken back,
what love couldn't recapture.
Now less than a silhouette
grown into the parrot perch,
this one died looking up at the sky.

Facing It

My black face fades,
hiding inside the black granite.
I said I wouldn't,
dammit: No tears.
I'm stone. I'm flesh.
My clouded reflection eyes me
like a bird of prey, the profile of night
slanted against morning. I turn
this way—the stone lets me go.
I turn that way—I'm inside
the Vietnam Veterans Memorial
again, depending on the light
to make a difference.
I go down the 58,022 names,
half-expecting to find
my own in letters like smoke.
I touch the name Andrew Johnson;
I see the booby trap's white flash.
Names shimmer on a woman's blouse
but when she walks away
the names stay on the wall.
Brushstrokes flash, a red bird's
wings cutting across my stare.
The sky. A plane in the sky.
A white vet's image floats
closer to me, then his pale eyes
look through mine. I'm a window.
He's lost his right arm
inside the stone. In the black mirror
a woman's trying to erase names:
No, she's brushing a boy's hair.

Neon
Vernacular

from *February in Sydney*

The Plea

Round about midnight
    the clock's ugly stare
hangs in mental repose
    & its antimagnetic second hand
measures a man's descent.
    Bop, bop, bebop, rebop.
The bottom falls out
    of each dream—
the silver spike is
    in my hands & I'm on the floor.
The Alice in Malice
    does a little soft shoe
on my troubled heart.
    Hot & heavy,
cool & cosmic honeydripper
    fingers play the missing notes
inbetween life & death
    round midnight.
Bop, bop, bebop, rebop.
    Lost lovers in my empty doorway
groove to a sweet pain
    in the bruise-colored neon
where my soul weaves
    itself into *terra incognita*,
into the blue & green
    sounds of Botany Bay
reflected like rozellas
    through the big, black
slow dance of waves grinding against the shore.
    Bop, bop, bebop, rebop.
Thelonious & bright as that
    golden plea of gospel
under everything
    Monk wrung from the keys.
Round about midnight
    despair returns each minute
like a drop of moonshine
    elongating into rapture
moaned through Bird's mouthpiece
    in a soundproof room

where trust & love
　　is white dust on the dark
furniture. Time is nothing
　　but an endless bridge.
All those who thought
　　they could use my body
for nowhere's roadmap
　　I see their blank faces
float up from a whirlpool
　　as the turntable spins.
Bop, bop, bebop, rebop.
　　Each undying note
resounds in my head;
　　there's a cry in every pocket
& low swell of unhappy
　　lust I've suffered,
& round about midnight the odor of sex
　　& salvation quivers in each song
the wooden hammers
　　strike from wire strings
like anger stolen back
　　from the soil.

The Man Who Carries the Desert
Around Inside Himself: For Wally

Desert dreamer, telepathic
sleepwalker over shifting sand,
your grandfather's on the last postcard
I airmailed to my mother.
Though he sees truer than you
this grog-scented night,
you remain in that skull-white landscape
like a figure burned into volcanic rock.
Reading footprints, straining not to walk
out of your body, you leave
a piece of yourself everywhere
you go, following some explorer's
sluggish boots like a slowmotion machine
stamping its imprint.
No rain for years, still
the labyrinth takes you home
to Alice Springs where gods
speak through blue-tongue lizards
& lost people become vivid
as Nosepeg's song cycles,
beyond wind-carved dunes
like humpback whales on the seafloor.
Atrocities of brightness
grow into a map of deaths
spread out like stars
as you read the debris
left by the sun & crows
where secret campsites
show through porcupine grass.
A cutting wind rides you down
like bushrangers, but you know
how to wrap your arms around
an anthill holding the midday
inside. Out of nothing
a slow rain glistens against silence
whispering to ghosts. Now
it's safe to cry away anger.

For you, the city's skyline
extends a lifetime into night.
Like spontaneous combustion, already
a wildfire of flowers
marches over the sand.

Rocks Push

A drizzle hangs in the air
like a torn photograph
of three of four tough guys
pieced together inside my head.
They ease up from the emulsion
of silver halides, with faith
in what lives under the whitewash
brushed over plague buildings.

Rocks Push, razor gang—
my imagination fires up
its black engine, & the car
creeping down a sidestreet
doesn't exist if I say so.
A foghorn shatters the stillness.
Everything's covered by a fine mist
from Fort Denison to the Observatory.

Faces play hide & seek, white & wet
as sandblasted gargoyles peering out of
the heart's rainy darkness.
Outside The Lord Nelson,
the night's festooned with play things
that swallow a man's spirit
& leave him dancing with silhouettes
till he falls drunk among roses.

Streetlights burn gauzy
& dim as Hell's Kitchen.
Cockney accents come with the wind.
I'm ready to turn my pockets inside out
& tell them I'm broke, that I'm as poor
& alone. Unwanted,
& a need to prove something to
women with corsets thrown on beds

lit by oil lamps, they bring back
trophies & stories of another's fear.
Did they foresee the flash of butterfly
knives in the hands of skinheads

bludgeoning the western suburbs?
East End
    Blackpool
        Woolloomooloo,
each blade sings about desire.

Laughing, with a TV's blue-static figures
   dancing through the air at 2 A.M.
with eight empty beer bottles lined up
   on the kitchen table, a full moon
gazing through the opened back door,
   his thick fingers drumming the pink
laminex, singing along with a rock video
   of soft porno, recounting dead friends,
with a tally of all his mistakes
   in front of him, after he's punched
the walls & refrigerator with his fist,
   unable to forget childhood's lonely
grass & nameless flowers & insects,
   crying for his black cat
hit by a car, drawing absent faces
   on the air with his right index finger,
rethinking lost years of a broken marriage
   like a wrecked ship inside a green bottle,
puffing a horn-shaped ceramic pipe,
   dragging his feet across the floor
in a dance with the shadow of a tree
   on a yellow wall, going to the wooden fence
to piss under the sky's marsupial stare,
   walking back in to pop the cap
on his last beer, hugging himself awake,
   picking up a dried wishbone
from the table & snapping it, cursing the world,
   softly whispering his daughter's name,
he disturbs the void that is
   heavy as the heart's clumsy logbook.

A Quality of Light

Two women in their twenties do a drunken
waltz. One wears a black
dress, opalescent under
the afternoon's ultraviolet,
& the other is in a see-
through sheath, curved
against the weak cloth,
crying, "Oh, is the Pope
here? Is he? Is he here?"
Four motorcycle cops
speed to a halt in shiny
leather & chrome glare.
She moves to a music
we touch in ourselves
sometimes, with her friend
shadowing her like a half-
forgotten thought. The sky
gleams off pails filled
with fresh-cut flowers.
Shopkeepers leave unbagged
apples & uncrated pears
to ripen in their sweet skins.

Italian,
Spanish, Greek.
Her white dress
sways in the heat,
merging with the Pope's
robe like metaphysics
& flesh. Innocence,
vulgarity, temptation,
spectacle, or what?
Hours later in bed,
I strain to hear him
say the word *Peace*
from his bulletproof
Popemobil, but only
the moon peers around
a corner of the window-
shade, transparent
as the dress, like a page
held up to sunlight
till it burns.

Gerry's Jazz

At fourteen you crawl through a hole
in the wall where they slip sly grog
into Ollie Ward's Maxine Cabaret,
& listen to a band play for gangsters.
You're on your way to Tom Ugly's
& El Rocco, & the guns on tables

can't stop you. Something
takes back part of childhood pain,
riding out long hours behind the trap
as the sonorous high hat
clicks a fraction between the cracks,
& then you're off on a trip:

Gene Krupa's *Wire Brush Stomp*
rains over the kit + sizzles like a tinroof
after you hired a blacksmith
to hammer a cymbol into shape.
You rap sticks against it & sound travels
through everyone like rings of water.

Cocky & skillful, you go
into a groove & dance the true pivot,
playing for jitterbug
contests at Katoomba & the Trocadero.
Going deeper into each song,
you rattle keys like Houdini locked in a trunk,

bending within a black echo.
"The difference
between the difference
is the difference," you holler
to a full moon hanging over
the steel mills of Wollongong.

Like an unknown voice rising
out of flesh, each secret
is buried beneath the skin,
& you feel they try to pick

your brain for them, to find
the rhythm of your heart,

as you swear the beat is stolen from the sea.
With empty flagons beside you at Fisherman's Bay,
you pat *Out of the Afternoon* upon your leg,
knowing you'll ride hope
till it's nothing but a shiny bone
under heavy light.

Boxing Day

> *"Burns never landed a blow.*
> *It was hopeless, preposterous, heroic."*
> —Jack London

This is where Jack Johnson
cornered Tommy Burns in 1908.
Strong as an ironbark
tree, he stood there
flexing his biceps
till he freed
the prisoner under his skin.
      The bell clanged
      & a profusion of voices
      shook the afternoon. Johnson
      jabbed with the power
      of an engine throwing a rod,
      & Burns sleepwalked
      to the spinning edge
of the planet like a moth
drawn to a burning candle.
He was dizzy as a drunken girl
tangoing with a flame tree
breaking into full bloom,
burdened by fruits of desire
& the smell of carnival.
      A currawong crossed the sun
      singing an old woman's cry.
      The referee threw in his towel
      in the fourteenth round & bookies
      scribbled numbers beside names
      madly, as twenty thousand rose
      into the air like a wave.
For years the razor-gang boys
bragged about how they would've KOed
Johnson, dancing & punching each day.
Eighty years later, the stadium's
checkered with tennis courts,
a plantation of pale suits
called White City.

I hear Miles Davis' trumpet
& Leadbelly's "Titanic."
A bell's metal treble
reverberates . . . the sunset
moves like a tremble of muscle
across Rushcutters Bay,
back to the name Johnson
flashing over the teletype
when he danced The Eagle Rock,
drove fast cars & had a woman
on each arm, to Jesse Willard
pushing him down into a whirlpool's
death roll under white
confetti & cheers in Havana.

Protection of Movable Cultural Heritage

Time-polished skulls of Yagan & Pemulwy
sit in a glass cage wired to a burglar alarm
in Britain, but the jaws of these two
resistance leaders haven't been broken
into a lasting grin for the empire.

Under fluorescent lamps they're crystal balls
into which one can gaze & see the past.
With eyes reflected into empty sockets
through the glass, I can't stop reading
an upside-down newspaper

headlining Klaus Barbie, Karl Linnas
& Bernhard Goetz. The skulls sit
like wax molds for Fear & Anger—
beheaded body-songs lament & recall
how windy grass once sang to the feet.

Now, staring from their display case,
they still govern a few broken hearts
wandering across the Nullarbor Plain.
Killed fighting for love of birthplace
under a sky ablaze with flying foxes

& shiny crows, they remember the weight
of chains inherited from the fathers
of bushrangers, how hatred runs into
the soul like red veins in the eye
or thin copper threads through money.

Blue Light Lounge Sutra for the
Performance Poets at Harold Park Hotel

the need gotta be
so deep words can't
answer simple questions
all night long notes
stumble off the tongue
& color the air indigo
so deep fragments of gut
& flesh cling to the song
you gotta get into it
so deep salt crystalizes on eyelashes
the need gotta be
so deep you can vomit up ghosts
& not feel broken
till you are no more
than a half ounce of gold
in painful brightness
you gotta get into it
blow that saxophone
so deep all the sex & dope in this world
can't erase your need
to howl against the sky
the need gotta be
so deep you can't
just wiggle your hips
& rise up out of it
chaos in the cosmos
modern man in the pepperpot
you gotta get hooked
into every hungry groove
so deep the bomb locked
in rust opens like a fist
into it into it so deep
rhythm is pre-memory

the need gotta be basic
animal need to see
& know the terror
we are made of honey
cause if you wanna dance
this boogie be ready
to let the devil use your head
for a drum

February in Sydney

Dexter Gordon's tenor sax
plays "April in Paris"
inside my head all the way back
on the bus from Double Bay.
Round Midnight, the '50s,
cool cobblestone streets
resound footsteps of Bebop
musicians with whiskey-laced voices
from a boundless dream in French.
Bud, Prez, Webster, & The Hawk,
their names run together riffs.
Painful gods jive talk through
bloodstained reeds & shiny brass
where music is an anesthetic.
Unreadable faces from the human void
float like torn pages across the bus
windows. An old anger drips into my throat,
& I try thinking something good,
letting the precious bad
settle to the salty bottom.
Another scene keeps repeating itself:
I emerge from the dark theatre,
passing a woman who grabs her red purse
& hugs it to her like a heart attack.
Tremolo. Dexter comes back to rest
behind my eyelids. A loneliness
lingers like a silver needle
under my black skin,
as I try to feel how it is
to scream for help through a horn.